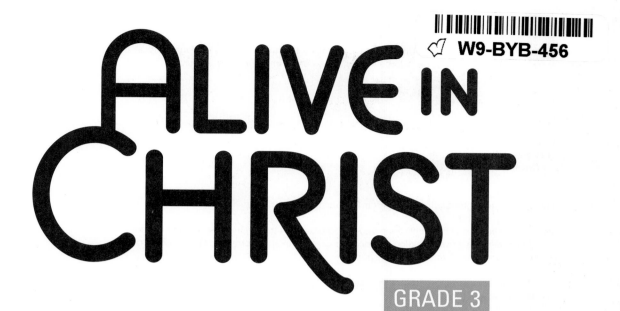

ALIVE IN CHRIST

GRADE 3

The Church

aliveinchrist.osv.com

Our Sunday Visitor

The Subcommittee on the Catechism, United States Conference of Catholic Bishops, has found this catechetical series, copyright 2014, to be in conformity with the *Catechism of the Catholic Church*.

Nihil Obstat
Rev. Fr. Jeremiah L. Payne, S.Th.L.
Censor Librorum, Diocese of Orlando

Imprimatur
✠ Most Rev. John Noonan
Bishop of Orlando
March 26, 2013

For permission to reprint copyrighted materials, grateful acknowledgment is made to the following sources:

English translation of the *Catechism of the Catholic Church for the United States of America* copyright © 1994, United States Catholic Conference, Inc.—Libreria Editrice Vaticana. English translation of the *Catechism of the Catholic Church: Modifications from the Editio Typica* copyright © 1997, United States Catholic Conference, Inc.—Libreria Editrice Vaticana. Used by permission. All rights reserved.

The English translation of a Psalm Response from *Lectionary for Mass* © 1969, 1981, 1997, International Commission on English in the Liturgy Corporation (ICEL); excerpts from the English translation of *Rite of Penance* © 1974, ICEL; excerpts from the English translation of *Pastoral Care of the Sick: Rites of Anointing and Viaticum* © 1982, ICEL; excerpts from the English translation of *Rite of Christian Initiation of Adults* © 1985, ICEL; excerpts from the English translation of *The Roman Missal* © 2010, ICEL. All rights reserved. Published with the approval of the Committee on Divine Worship, United States Conference of Catholic Bishops.

Excerpts from the *United States Catholic Catechism for Adults,* copyright © 2006, United States Catholic Conference, Inc.—Libreria Editrice Vaticana.

Music selections copyrighted or administered by OCP Publications are used with permission of OCP Publications, 5536 NE Hassalo, Portland, OR 97213. Please refer to songs for specific copyright dates and information.

Scripture selections taken from the *New American Bible, revised edition* © 2010, 1991, 1986, 1970 by the Confraternity of Christian Doctrine, Washington, D.C., and are used by license of the copyright owner. All rights reserved. No part of the *New American Bible* may be reproduced in any form without permission in writing from the copyright owner.

Additional acknowledgments appear on page 336.

Alive in Christ Parish Grade 3 Student Book
ISBN: 978-1-61278-010-8
Item Number: CU5100

2 3 4 5 6 7 8 9 015016 19 18 17 16 15
Webcrafters, Inc., Madison, WI, USA; March 2015; Job# 120553

Contents at a Glance

© Our Sunday Visitor

Contents in Detail

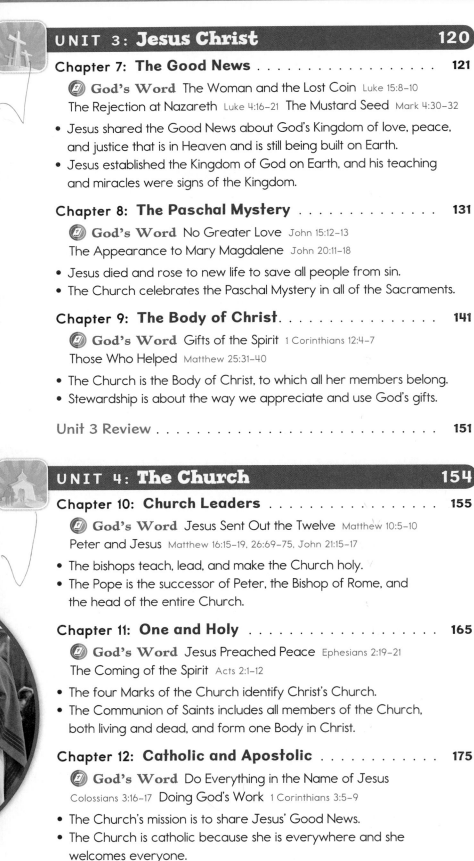

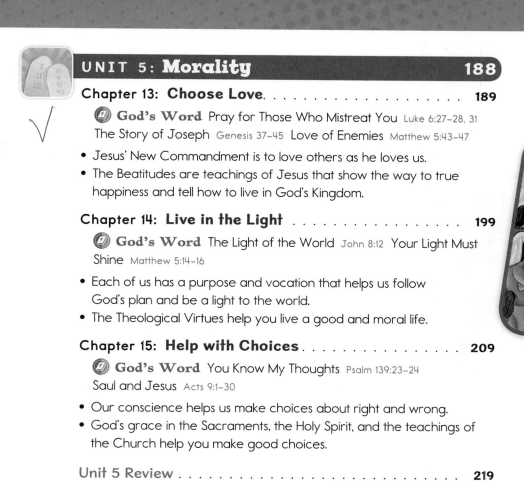

A New Year

 ## Let Us Pray

Leader: Father, you call us together as your Church. You give us your Son to teach and lead us, and your Spirit to make us one.

"*Hallelujah!*
Sing to the LORD a new song,
his praise in the assembly of the faithful...
For the LORD takes delight in his
people..." Psalm 149:1, 4

All: God, thank you for uniting us. Give us life and love as we grow as the Body of Christ on Earth. Amen.

God's Word

"For all of you who were baptized into Christ have clothed yourselves with Christ. There is neither Jew nor Greek, there is neither slave nor free person, there is not male and female; for you are all one in Christ Jesus." Galatians 3:27-28

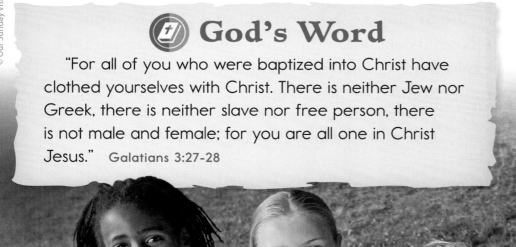

What Do You Wonder?

- How are we one in Christ?
- What makes us the Church?

Third Grade

What's going to happen this year?

This year is all about learning, loving, and celebrating our Catholic faith!

When you see , you know it's a story or reading from the Bible. You will spend lots of time with God's Word from the Bible. Through Bible stories, you will discover more about being a follower of Christ and member of the Church.

When you see ♥, you know it's time to pray. Each time you are together, you have the chance to listen to and talk to God in prayer. You will grow closer as a community as you pray together and get to know Jesus' teachings.

When you see ▶, you will sing songs to praise God and celebrate your faith. During the year you'll explore the Church's feasts and seasons, and meet many Saints, our heroes of the Church.

⭐ **Circle two things you will do this year.**

This gold star begins an activity to help you better understand what's being taught. You may underline, circle, write, match, or draw.

A Community of Faith

This year you will learn a lot about the **Church**, the community of all baptized who believe in God and follow Jesus Christ. Important words like this are **highlighted** in yellow so you don't miss them.

You'll get a deeper understanding of what it means to belong to the Catholic Church. You will explore how the Church is the Body of Christ whose various members work together to share the Good News of Jesus and give thanks through worship and prayer.

Catholic Faith Words

In this box you will again see the **highlighted** words and definitions.

Church the community of all baptized people who believe in God and follow Jesus; the word is often used for the Catholic Church because she traces her origins back to the Apostles

Share Your Faith

When you see these fun green words, you know it's time for an activity!

Think What words would you use to describe the Church?

_____

_____

Share Talk with a partner about your words and what it means to belong to the Church.

God's Word

Where can you read stories about God?

The **Bible** is a holy book. It is God's Word written down by humans. The word Bible means "books." Many different books are included in the Bible. The Bible has two main parts, the Old Testament and the New Testament.

The Bible is also called Scripture, which means "writing." We hear readings from Scripture during Mass and the other Sacraments.

The Old Testament

The Old Testament tells the story of the Hebrew people and their covenant with God.

Catholic Faith Words

Bible the Word of God written in human words. The Bible is the Holy Book of the Church.

Old Testament

- The stories of Adam and Eve, Noah, Abraham and Sarah, Moses, Joseph and his brothers, and King David are in the Old Testament.
- These stories tell you about your ancestors in faith.
- The Church reads from the Old Testament at most Masses.

The New Testament

The New Testament tells the story of our faith since Jesus was born. It is about the life and teaching's of Jesus, his followers, and the early Church.

New Testament

- The first four books are called the Gospels. They tell about Jesus' life on Earth and how he died and rose to save us.

- A book called the Acts of the Apostles tells how the Church grew after Jesus returned to his Father.

- Epistles, or letters, from Saint Paul and other Church leaders tell Jesus' followers how to live their faith.

- The Book of Revelation tells what will happen at the end of time, when Jesus comes again in glory.

Connect Your Faith

 God's Word

"I am the light of the world. Whoever follows me will not walk in darkness, but will have the light of life." John 8:12

Verse

Chapter Number

Book Name

Find the Bible Passage Find the Bible passage in Chapter 5, page 97 and write the book name, chapter number, and verse.

Book Name: _____

Chapter Number: _____   Verse: _____

Our Catholic Life

What does it mean to be Catholic?

Each chapter in your book has an Our Catholic Life section. It shows in a special way what it means to be Catholic. Words, pictures, and activities help us grow closer to Jesus and the Church.

Grow as a Follower of Jesus

- know more about our faith
- learn about the Sacraments
- live as Jesus taught us
- talk and listen to God in prayer
- take part in Church life
- help others know Jesus through what we say and do

People of Faith

You will also meet People of Faith, holy women and men who loved God very much and did his work on Earth.

Live Your Faith

Spread the Good News! Write one thing about Jesus that you can share with someone you know.

_____

Write one question you have about Jesus or the Church.

_____

 **Let Us Pray**

Pray Together

Every chapter has a prayer page, with lots of different ways to pray. You may listen to God's Word read from the Bible, pray for the needs of others, call on the Saints to pray for us, and praise God the Father, Son, and Holy Spirit in words and songs.

Gather and begin with the Sign of the Cross.

Leader: Blessed be God.

All: Blessed be God forever.

Leader: Let us pray.

Bow your head as the leader prays.

All: Amen.

Leader: A reading from the holy Gospel according to John.
Read John 15:1–8.
The Gospel of the Lord.

All: Praise to you, Lord Jesus Christ.

 Sing "Alive in Christ"
We are Alive in Christ
We are Alive in Christ
He came to set us free
We are Alive in Christ
We are Alive in Christ
He gave his life for me
We are Alive in Christ
We are Alive in Christ

FAMILY+FAITH
LIVING AND LEARNING TOGETHER

YOUR CHILD LEARNED >>>

This page is for you, the parent, to encourage you to talk about your faith and see the many ways you already live your faith in daily family life.

In this section, you will find a summary of what your child has learned in the chapter.

God's Word

 In this section, you will find a Scripture citation and a summary of what your child has learned in the chapter.

Catholics Believe

• Bulleted information highlights the main points of doctrine in the Chapter.

Here you will find chapter connections to the *Catechism of the Catholic Church.*

People of Faith

Here you meet the holy person featured in People of Faith.

CHILDREN AT THIS AGE >>>

This feature gives you a sense of how your child, at this particular age, will likely be able to understand what is being taught. It suggests ways you can help your child better understand, live, and love their faith.

How They Understand Your third-grader is beginning to identify him or her self, and others, as members of groups. At this age, they begin to be joiners. They like communal activities such as team sports, hobby clubs, and scouting. Your family and parish community will still be a strong influence for your son or daughter.

For eight or nine year olds, putting someone else's needs ahead of their own is a new concept. They are just learning how to be unselfish. Help them see how Jesus ignored his own comfort to help others.

Find opportunities to affirm your child or other children when they show consideration for others, patience in a difficult situation, and courage in the face of teasing.

CONSIDER THIS >>>

This section includes a question that invites you to reflect on your own experience and consider how the Church speaks to you on your own faith journey.

LET'S TALK >>>

• Here you will find some practical questions that prompt discussion about the lesson's content, faith sharing, and making connections with your family life.

• Ask your child to share one thing they've learned about their book.

LET'S PRAY >>>

 This section encourages family prayer connected to the example of our People of Faith.

Holy men and women, pray for us. Amen.

 For a multimedia glossary of Catholic Faith Words, Sunday readings, seasonal and Saint resources, and chapter activities go to **aliveinchrist.osv.com**.

All Saints and All Souls

 Let Us Pray

Leader: Dear Jesus, I trust in you. I know you are with me now. You will always be with me. Guide me to stay on your path every day.

"To you, O LORD, I lift up my soul, my God, in you I trust."   Psalm 25:1-2

All: Amen.

God's Word

Amen, amen, I say to you, unless a grain of wheat falls to the ground and dies, it remains just a grain of wheat; but if it dies, it produces much fruit.... Whoever serves me must follow me, and where I am, there also will my servant be. The Father will honor whoever serves me.   John 12:24, 26

? What Do You Wonder?

- What makes a grain of wheat grow and bear fruit?

- How many ways can you serve Jesus?

Mexico's Día de los Muertos celebrates and honors all the dead with a special focus on ancestors. Families visit the gravesites of their departed loved ones.

The Feast of All Saints

- The feast of All Saints is celebrated on November 1. The day after, November 2, is the feast of All Souls.

- These feasts honor the people who have died and gone before us. Many parishes remember those who have died all month.

Remembering the Dead

The Church has two special days for remembering people who have died. Both of the days are in November. On November 1, we celebrate All Saints Day. We honor everyone who is in Heaven. We honor these people, the Saints, even though we only know the names of some of them. On November 2, we celebrate All Souls Day. We pray for people who have died but who are not in Heaven yet. They are in Purgatory.

In some cultures, All Souls Day is very important. It is an occasion to remember that people on Earth and their relatives in Heaven remain united through prayer. For instance, many Latinos in the United States and in Latin America celebrate El Día de los Muertos (The Day of the Dead). On that day, graves of their relatives are decorated with flowers. They eat special foods. They also make a family altar. Candles and pictures are on the altar. Families gather at the altar and say prayers for their relatives.

➡ How does your parish remember those who have died?

These feasts help us remember that people who have died are very much part of the Church. They are part of the Communion of Saints. You honor the Saints and pray for those in Purgatory.

A Saint is...

Saints are heroes of the Church who loved God very much, led a holy life, and are now with God in Heaven. We know the names of some of the Saints, but there are many Saints we do not know. We remember all of them on All Saints Day when we honor all of those who opened their lives to God on Earth and are enjoying life forever with God in Heaven. We can also ask patron Saints to pray for us about specific things. They are connected in a special way to a place, person, or type of work.

Activity

Find a Patron Saint There is a patron Saint for almost anything you can think of, like Saint Cecilia, the patron Saint of music, or Saint Albert, the patron Saint of scientists and students. Think of some things you like to do or that are most important to you. Research the name of the patron Saint for these subjects and write their names below.

_____

_____

_____

_____

_____

_____

People of Faith

Chapter	Person	Feast Day
1	Blessed Rabanus Maurus	February 4
2	Saint Francis of Assisi	October 4
3	Blessed Luigi Betrame Quattrocchi and Blessed Maria Corsini	November 25
4	Saint John of Matha	February 8
5	Saint Mary MacKillop	August 8
6	Saint Gertrude the Great	November 16
7	Saint Isaac Jogues	October 19
8	Saint Mary Magdalene	July 22
9	Blessed Joseph Vaz	January 16
10	Saint Gregory the Great	September 3
11	Saints Perpetua and Felicity	March 7
12	Saint Elizabeth Ann Seton	January 4
13	Saint Peter Canisius	December 21
14	Saint Genevieve	January 3
15	Saint Pio (Padre Pio)	September 23
16	Saint John the Baptist	June 24
17	Saint Marianne Cope	January 23
18	Saint Jean-Baptiste de la Salle	April 7
19	Saint Clement of Rome	November 23
20	Saint Peter Claver	September 9
21	Saint Joseph	March 19

Saint Francis of Assisi

Saint Elizabeth Ann Seton

Saint Pio

♡ Let Us Pray

A Prayer for the Dead

Gather and begin with the Sign of the Cross.

Leader: Let us pray to God, that we may honor members of our families and everyone else who have died, we pray,

All: Lord of Life, hear our prayer.

Leader: That we may carry on the good work they have done, we pray,

All: Lord of Life, hear our prayer.

Leader: That we will remember all those who have died and have no one to pray for them,

All: Lord of Life, hear our prayer.

Leader: That those who were victims of natural disasters will know peace and life with God forever, we pray,

All: Lord of Life, hear our prayer.

Leader: That all the dead who suffered enjoy the happiness of your love in Heaven, we pray,

All: Lord of Life, hear our prayer.

Leader: Give them eternal rest, O Lord.

All: And may your light shine on them forever.

FAMILY+FAITH
LIVING OUR CATHOLIC FAITH

TALKING ABOUT ORDINARY TIME >>>

On the Feast of All Saints we honor all the Saints. We honor the many people who are in Heaven because they responded to God's grace and lived according to the Gospel. For this feast on November 1 and the feast of All Souls on November 2, we remember those in Purgatory. Catholics believe that those who die in God's friendship but who are not completely purified need purification in Purgatory before enjoying Heaven. As a member of the Communion of Saints, you are encouraged by the Church to pray for the souls in Purgatory.

God's Word

 Read **John 12:23-28** part of Jesus' farewell conversation with his disciples before his death. It focuses on his death but also refers to us and the dying and new life we experience.

HELPING YOUR CHILD UNDERSTAND >>>

Death

- Most children this age understand that when a person dies they permanently leave this Earth.

- At this age many children have some fear and anxiety that people they love and who love and care for them will die.

- In most cases children are comforted by the faith of the Church which tells us that there is life after death.

CATHOLIC FAMILY CUSTOMS >>>

Prayer Space Create a family prayer space as a memorial during November. Place in such space pictures of relatives who have died. Consider lighting a candle for them during family prayer time.

Refer to departed relatives on family occasions during November. For example, sing one of their favorite hymns during family prayers, or add one of their favorite foods to an All Souls Day dinner.

FAMILY PRAYER >>>

 Use this prayer at family gatherings in November.

Dear God, You have made us a family.
Some of our members are no longer with us.
We know that they live in you.
We know that they praise you.
We offer our prayers for their souls.
We look forward to being united with them in Heaven.

We pray this through Jesus, your Son. Amen.

For a multimedia glossary of Catholic Faith Words, Sunday readings, seasonal and Saint resources, and chapter activities go to **aliveinchrist.osv.com**.

Walk in the Light

 ## Let Us Pray

Leader: Lord God of Light,
open my eyes to see you more clearly.
Bring light to my Advent path.

"…let us walk in the light of the LORD!"
Isaiah 2:5b

All: Amen.

God's Word

"…the night is advanced, the day is at hand. Let us then throw off the works of darkness [and] put on the armor of light; let us conduct ourselves properly as in the day…" Romans 13:12-13a

? What Do You Wonder?

- What do we act like when we walk in the dark?
- What is different when we act in the light?

Jesus, God's Light

Advent is the first season of the Church year. As you prepare your heart for the coming of Jesus' Kingdom, you pray for his light to help you choose right actions. You ask him to make your heart ready for when he comes again at the end of time.

Long before Jesus was born, God's people waited for a Savior to bring God's light. They "walked in darkness" (Isaiah 9:1). When the time was right, God sent his Son, God's own Light, into the world to be our Savior.

Advent helps you remember that Jesus is the light in your life, too. The Advent wreath reminds you to prepare your heart to welcome Jesus. The Advent wreath has four candles. A candle is lit each week during Advent. A special prayer is prayed to ask that the light of Jesus come into your life.

➜ **What does your family do during Advent?**

Underline what the Advent wreath prepares you to do.

Lighting the Advent Wreath

- We light purple candles on the first and second Sundays of Advent.

- On the third Sunday, we also light the rose colored candle as a sign of joy and rejoicing. Our wait for Christmas is almost over.

- On the fourth Sunday, we add the last purple candle so all are lit.

 **Let Us Pray**

Witness to the Light

Gather and begin with the Sign of the Cross.

Leader: Our help is in the name of the Lord.

All: Who made Heaven and Earth.

Leader: Let us pray.
Bow your heads as the leader prays.

All: Amen.

Listen to God's Word

Reader: A reading from the holy Gospel according to John.
Read John 1:6–9.
The Gospel of the Lord.

All: Praise to you, Lord Jesus Christ.

Go Forth!

Leader: Jesus, Light of the World, we ask you to bring your
healing light to those for whom we now pray.

 All: Sing "Jambo, Jesu (Hello, Jesus)"

Lord of all life, be with us.
Lord of all life, be with us.
Lord of all life, be with us.
Lord of all life, be near.

Text: Refrain based on African Prayer, "Lord of All Life" Text and music © 1995,
Jack Miffleton. Published by OCP. All rights reserved.

FAMILY+FAITH

LIVING AND LEARNING TOGETHER

TALKING ABOUT ADVENT >>>

Advent is the first four weeks of the Church year. The physical darkness we experience during these short December days symbolizes the spiritual darkness of the time before Christ's birth. During the four weeks of Advent, the priest wears purple vestments. Purple is the color of royalty as we await the coming King. It is also the color for mourning and penance.

God's Word

 Read **Romans 13:12-13** to find how Paul encouraged early Christians to live by Jesus' Greatest and New Commandment.

HELPING YOUR CHILD UNDERSTAND >>>

Advent

- Typically at this age children are beginning to understand the consequences of being ready or not being ready on time.

- Usually they need some help expanding their concrete experiences of darkness and light to encompass abstract meanings of darkness and light.

- Help your child recall a time when they or you were able to make someone who was sad or lonely smile.

FEASTS OF THE SEASON >>>

Feast of Saint Lucy
December 13

Her name means light. On her feast, Scandinavian people practice the custom of processions led by one girl wearing a crown of candles (or lights), while others in the procession hold only a single candle each. All bring treats to be shared.

FAMILY PRAYER >>>

Jesus, we are waiting for you to come into our hearts. Help us prepare for you by helping others. Let us share your light by serving others. Amen.

For a multimedia glossary of Catholic Faith Words, Sunday readings, seasonal and Saint resources, and chapter activities go to **aliveinchrist.osv.com**.

Our Lady of Guadalupe

 ## Let Us Pray

Leader: Dear Lady of Guadalupe,

Mother of Jesus and our Mother, teach us your ways of gentleness and strength. Guide us to help those experiencing great needs. Hear our prayer.

"Sing a new song to the LORD,
 for he has done marvelous deeds." **Psalm 98:1a**

All: Amen.

God's Word

And Mary said: "My soul proclaims the greatness of the Lord; my spirit rejoices in God my savior. For he has looked upon his handmaid's lowliness; behold, from now on will all ages call me blessed. The Mighty One has done great things for me, and holy is his name. His mercy is from age to age to those who respect him."

Based on Luke 1:46-50

? What Do You Wonder?

• How do you reflect God's goodness with your actions?

• What makes other people happy with God's gifts?

The Blessed Mother

Early one morning in December, a Nahuatl Indian named Juan Diego heard the beautiful sound of singing birds. He heard someone call his name, "Juanito," (little Juan). There he saw a beautiful young woman. She told him she was the Virgin Mary. She wanted Juan Diego to tell the bishop of Mexico to build a temple on the hill to honor her.

When Juan Diego gave the bishop Mary's message, the bishop did not believe him and asked him for some proof. Later, Mary appeared to Juan Diego again and told him to go up the hill where he would find roses. It was almost impossible for roses to grow in December. He went up the hill and found beautiful roses, cut them, and put them in his cloak. He returned to the bishop with the flowers. When Juan Diego opened his cloak, roses fell onto the floor and Our Lady of Guadalupe miraculously appeared.

➡ **What was special about the roses that Juan Diego found and presented to the bishop?**

Advent Feasts

- During the four weeks of Advent, the Church celebrates two very special feasts of Mary.

- December 8 is the feast of the Immaculate Conception of Mary. December 12 is the feast of Our Lady of Guadalupe.

Our Lady of Guadalupe

This prayer form is called a litany which is a prayer of petition that repeats a line several times.

 Let Us Pray

Gather and begin with the Sign of the Cross.

Leader: The Lord be with you.

All: And with your spirit.

Leader: Lord, have mercy on us.

All: Christ, have mercy on us.

Leader: Lord, have mercy on us. Christ hear us.

All: Christ, graciously hear us.

Leader: Our Lady of Guadalupe,

All: Pray for us.

Leader: Mother of those who suffer,

All: Pray for us.

Leader: Patroness of the Americas,

All: Pray for us.

Leader: Mother of all peoples around the world,

All: Pray for us.

Leader: Pray for us, O holy Mother of God.

All: That we may be made worthy of the promises of Christ. Amen.

FAMILY+FAITH
LIVING AND LEARNING TOGETHER

TALKING ABOUT ADVENT >>>

Mary, the Mother of God, is a prominent figure in the Advent season. During the Sundays of Advent we hear the stories of the Annunciation. The Angel Gabriel tells Mary she is to be the Mother of God's only Son. We also hear about Mary's visit to her cousin Elizabeth when she sings her song of praise and thanks in the *Magnificat*. In these four weeks, the Church also celebrates two very special feasts of Mary. December 8 is the feast of the Immaculate Conception of Mary. This feast honors Mary because she was born without Original Sin. It is a holy day of obligation. December 12 is the feast of Our Lady of Guadalupe. Blessed Pope John Paul II named Our Lady of Guadalupe the Patroness of the Americas. It is a holy day in the United States.

God's Word

 Read **Luke 1:26-38**, the story of the Annunciation and Mary's response to serve God.

HELPING YOUR CHILD UNDERSTAND >>>

Mary

- Most children this age will easily identify with Mary as a Mother and attribute to her the characteristics of a good mother.

- Usually they will accept without analysis that Mary is the Mother of the human Jesus and so the Mother of God.

- As a rule, they will be intrigued with different art forms of Mary.

FEASTS OF THE SEASON >>>

Feast of the Immaculate Conception of Mary
December 8

This feast honors Mary because she was born without Original Sin. It is a holy day of obligation. One of the cherished Sacramentals of Catholic devotion to Mary is the Miraculous Medal. The medal was described to Saint Catherine Laboure during an apparition of Mary. Inscribed on the medal are the words: "O Mary conceived without sin, pray for us who have recourse to thee."

FAMILY PRAYER >>>

 O God of power and mercy, you blessed the Americas with the presence of the Virgin Mary of Guadalupe. May her prayers help all people everywhere to accept each other as brothers and sisters. Through your justice present in our hearts, may your peace reign in our family, our neighborhood and the world.

We ask this through our Lord Jesus Christ, your Son, who lives and reigns with you and the Holy Spirit, One God, forever and ever. Amen.

For a multimedia glossary of Catholic Faith Words, Sunday readings, seasonal and Saint resources, and chapter activities go to **aliveinchrist.osv.com**.

Glory to God

 Let Us Pray

Leader: God, our Heavenly Father,
We praise and bless you for the gift of your Son
Jesus. He brings light and peace to our world. We
pray that all people of the world will know peace
in this season.

"Arise! Shine, for your light has come,
the glory of the LORD has dawned upon you."
Isaiah 60:1

All: Amen.

📖 God's Word

For a child is born to us, a son is given to us;
upon his shoulder dominion rests.
They name him Wonder-Counselor, God-Hero,
Father-Forever, Prince of Peace. Isaiah 9:5

? What Do You Wonder?

- What does it mean for dominion to rest on Jesus' shoulders?
- Which title is the best for Jesus?

Praise Jesus

At Christmas, the Church praises and thanks God for all his gifts, especially for the best gift of all—Jesus! We want to thank God for Jesus and for our many blessings. The Church gives God thanks and honors him in many ways.

The most important prayer of thanks and praise is the Mass. Beginning on Christmas Eve, special Masses are celebrated each day to worship God during the Christmas season. Displaying Nativity scenes is another way to praise God for the gift of Jesus.

➜ **What is your favorite way to thank and praise God in prayer?**

Circle the ways that we worship God during the Christmas season.

Christmas Day

On Christmas Day the Church gives God thanks and praise for Jesus' birth. The feast of Christmas begins a major season in the Church year. It is so important that the celebration starts in prayer on December 24, at the Christmas Eve Vigil. It continues for a few weeks until the feast of the Baptism of Jesus.

Cardinal Donald Wuerl blesses the altar.

God's Great Gift

God gives you a special gift in Jesus. You can give your own gifts to God. Your prayers of thanksgiving are your gifts. You can pray with words, gestures, and actions, during the Mass or at any time.

➤ **Have you seen other people pray in ways that are different from the way you pray?**

Activity

Prayer Journal Keep a prayer journal with your thoughts and feelings about God. Start today using the space below.

_____

_____

_____

_____

_____

_____

Celebrate Jesus

This form of prayer is the prayer of praise that Jesus taught us. We conclude our prayer sharing with each other a sign of peace.

 ## Let Us Pray

Gather and begin with the Sign of the Cross.

Leader: Blessed be the name of the Lord.

All: Now and for ever.

Leader: Let us pray.
Bow your heads as you praise God.

All: Amen.

Listen to God's Word

Leader: A reading from the holy Gospel according to Luke.
Read Luke 2:1–14.
The Gospel of the Lord.

All: Praise to you, Lord Jesus Christ.

Leader: At the Savior's command, we dare to say:

All: Our Father…

Leader: May the God of light and peace fill our hearts and lives.

All: Amen.

Leader: Let us offer each other the sign of peace.

Offer one another a sign of peace.

Go Forth!

Leader: Let us go forth this week to give thanks for God's gift of Jesus.

All: Thanks be to God.

 Sing "Hark, The Herald Angels Sing."

Hark! the herald angels sing:
"Glory to the newborn King;
Peace on earth, and mercy mild,
God and sinners reconciled!"
Joyful, all ye nations, rise,
join the triumph of the skies;
with angelic hosts proclaim:
"Christ is born in Bethlehem!"
Hark! the herald angels sing,
"Glory to the newborn King."

FAMILY+FAITH
LIVING AND LEARNING TOGETHER

TALKING ABOUT CHRISTMAS >>>

The Church considers most sacred the memorial of Christ's birth and the early manifestations of his birth. She celebrates the great mystery of God becoming man in Jesus Christ. While the day may be overshadowed with many activities in our society, the Church compels us to pay attention to the feast and the season. The season begins with the Vigil on Christmas Eve and ends on the Feast of the Baptism of Jesus. Throughout the season, we are greeted in our parishes with candles, carols, a Nativity Scene, and white or gold vestments. This is the season of light, hope, peace, and joy.

God's Word

 Read **Isaiah 9:1-6** to find the first reading for the Christmas Mass at Midnight. In it the prophet Isaiah describes what it will be like when the Messiah comes.

HELPING YOUR CHILD UNDERSTAND >>>
Christmas

- The readings of the Christmas season will give you an opportunity to discuss God's command to love and serve others.

- By this age, children should know the protocol for thanking gift-givers and taking care of the gifts they receive. Encourage this practice. It strengthens the virtue of gratitude.

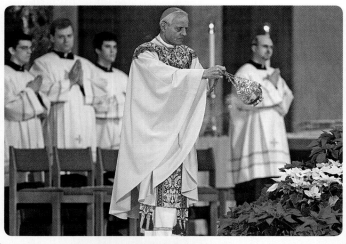

CATHOLIC FAMILY CUSTOMS >>>
Evergreen Wreaths

Evergreen wreaths and pine trees symbolize God's everlasting love for us. Take a family walk and collect pinecones and pine tree branches. During the Christmas season, place the pinecones and branches in the center of the dinner table as a reminder of God's love.

FAMILY PRAYER >>>

God of love, help us to live in love and unity as a family. Unite us in respect and peace. Grant this through our Lord Jesus Christ, your Son, who lives and reigns with you and the Holy Spirit, one God, for ever and ever. Amen.

For a multimedia glossary of Catholic Faith Words, Sunday readings, seasonal and Saint resources, and chapter activities go to **aliveinchrist.osv.com**.

Time for Change

♥ Let Us Pray

Leader: Lord, God, send your Holy Spirit to guide us in the ways of doing good and avoiding evil. Through Christ, our Lord.

"The LORD is my light and my salvation;
whom should I fear?

The LORD is my life's refuge;
of whom should I be afraid?" **Psalm 27:1**

All: Amen.

📖 God's Word

"And this is the verdict, that the light came into the world, but people preferred darkness to light, because their works were evil. For everyone who does wicked things hates the light and does not come toward the light, so that his works might not be exposed. But whoever lives the truth comes to the light, so that his works may be clearly seen as done in God."

John 3:19-21

❓ What Do You Wonder?

- Why do we call Jesus the "light"?
- Why do people do evil things?

Growing in Faith

To help you grow stronger as a follower of Christ, the Church gives you the forty days of Lent. During Lent you prepare your heart for the joy of Easter by the Lenten practices of fasting, prayer, and almsgiving. These practices help you show sorrow for your sins and the desire to do better.

Lenten Acts

To make yourself stronger, you might decide to give up certain treats or a favorite activity during Lent. You can use any money you save to remember the needs of others.

Your Lenten practice can also include positive actions. You can choose to pray more often, go to Mass more often, or go out of your way to do something good for others.

➤ **What will you do this Lent to grow closer to Jesus?**

Lent

- The season of Lent begins on Ash Wednesday and lasts for forty days.

- Purple, the color of Lent, reminds us that we need to repent.

- Lent is a season of change for the Church and her members.

Circle some things you can do to make yourself stronger during Lent.

More Like Jesus

The Cross is the sign of what Jesus was willing to do for all people. God loves us so much that he sent his Son whose death saved us from sin and eternal death.

Making the Sign of the Cross is a reminder of the sacrifice of love that was made for you by Jesus. It is also a reminder that you are his disciple. During Lent you and your faith community strive to become more like Jesus through prayer and helping others.

➔ **Who reminds you most of Jesus?**

➔ **How are you "like Jesus" for others each day?**

Decorate a Lenten Cross Decorate the cross and write Lenten words below that remind you of the extra things you are doing during Lent.

_____

_____

_____

Let Us Pray

Celebrate Lent

Gather and begin with the Sign of the Cross.

Leader: O Lord, open my lips.

All: That my mouth shall proclaim your praise.

Leader: Let us pray.

Bow your head as the leader prays.

All: Amen.

Listen to God's Word

Leader: A reading from the Letter to the Ephesians.
Read Ephesians 5:1–2, 8–10.
The Word of the Lord.

All: Thanks be to God.

Prayer of the Faithful

Leader: Let us pray. Lord Jesus, you promise that God, our Father, will hear our prayers. We pray those prayers now.

Respond to each prayer with these words.

All: Lord, hear our prayer.

Leader: At the Savior's command, we dare to say:

All: Our Father…

Go Forth!

Leader: Let us go forth this week to pray, sacrifice, and help others, remembering all that Jesus has done for us.

All: Thanks be to God.

 Sing "Lord, throughout These Holy Days"

FAMILY+FAITH
LIVING AND LEARNING TOGETHER

TALKING ABOUT LENT >>>

Lent is a forty day journey that begins on Ash Wednesday. The receiving of ashes on one's forehead marks one's promise to repent or change to grow closer to God and the Church. Lent is a time of inner change for us. Inspired by Jesus' time in the desert, we seek to change ourselves by taking away worldly distractions and practicing the Lenten disciplines of prayer, fasting, and doing penance.

God's Word

 Read **John 3:19-21** to see how Jesus responded to Nicodemus' questions about being "born again."

HELPING YOUR CHILD UNDERSTAND >>>
Lent

- Children this age often overestimate their ability to do things. They need to be helped to attempt small behavior changes.

- Since most children this age tend to respond to immediate gratification, forty days is a long time for them to be engaged in the same behaviors. Make a chart with forty days. Every ten days check in and see how your child is doing. Let him or her tell you on a scale of 1-10 how hard it is to keep this promise. Write the number on the calendar. Affirm his or her faithfulness.

FEASTS OF THE SEASON >>>
Feast of Annunciation
March 25

During this season we are reminded that Mary's "yes" to God's will was a gift for us. Her decision had eternal consequences: redemption for all.

FAMILY PRAYER >>>

 Set aside time before an evening meal to share a family prayer cup. Before you pass the family prayer cup, explain that you want to think about the season of Lent and what you are doing during Lent to grow closer to God. Pray the following prayer together.

Dear Jesus, may we follow your example during this season of Lent. As we drink from the family prayer cup, help us realize that you are always with us. Thank you for your help. Amen.

For a multimedia glossary of Catholic Faith Words, Sunday readings, seasonal and Saint resources, and chapter activities go to **aliveinchrist.osv.com**.

Holy Week

 Let Us Pray

Leader: Lord, God, we believe you will always love us.
Send your Holy Spirit to help us always love you.
Through Christ, our Lord,

"Forever I will maintain my mercy for him;
my covenant with him stands firm." **Psalm 89:29**

All: Amen.

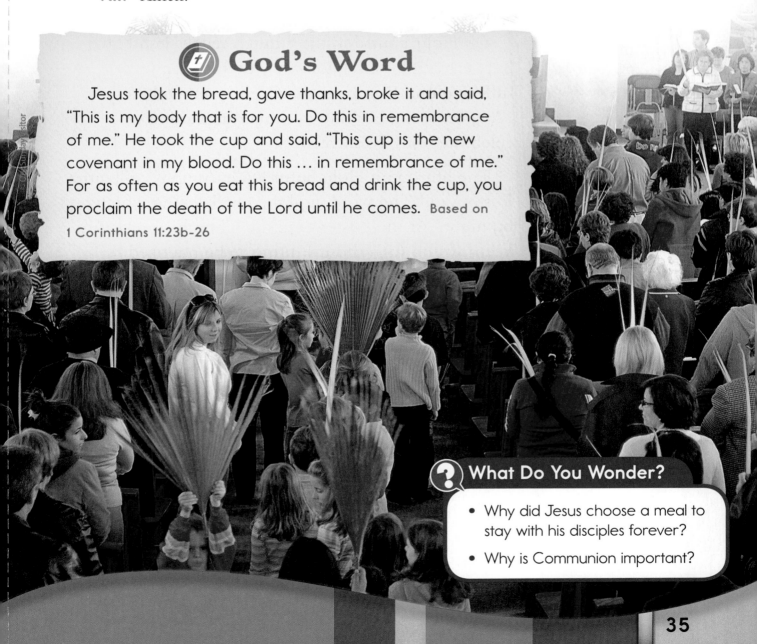

God's Word

Jesus took the bread, gave thanks, broke it and said, "This is my body that is for you. Do this in remembrance of me." He took the cup and said, "This cup is the new covenant in my blood. Do this … in remembrance of me." For as often as you eat this bread and drink the cup, you proclaim the death of the Lord until he comes. **Based on** 1 Corinthians 11:23b-26

? What Do You Wonder?

- Why did Jesus choose a meal to stay with his disciples forever?
- Why is Communion important?

35

Rejoice

At the end of Lent, the Church sets aside a very holy week. It begins on Palm Sunday with the procession of palms and reading of the Passion.

The last three days of Holy Week celebrate what Jesus did for all people. The Church calls these three special days the Triduum. The Triduum begins with the Holy Thursday Mass of the Lord's Supper and ends with evening prayer on Easter Sunday.

The Three Days

On Holy Thursday the Church recalls Jesus' Last Supper with his disciples. On Good Friday Jesus' suffering and Death on the Cross is remembered. Holy Saturday is a day of prayerful waiting to celebrate Jesus' Resurrection.

The liturgy on Holy Saturday evening is called the Easter Vigil. The word vigil means "keeping watch by night." At the Easter Vigil the Church community keeps watch with those waiting to be baptized.

To express the joy of Jesus' Resurrection, the deacon or other minister sings the Easter Proclamation.

➔ **What are some other ways people express joy in the Resurrection?**

Underline what the word vigil means.

© Our Sunday Visitor

On Palm Sunday palm branches are sprinkled with holy water and blessed before they are distributed to the assembly.

Let Us Pray

Celebrate Holy Week

Gather and begin with the Sign of the Cross.

Leader: O Lord, open my lips.

All: That my mouth shall proclaim your praise.

Leader: Let us pray.

Bow your head as the leader prays.

All: Amen.

Listen to God's Word

Reader: A reading from the Letter to the Romans.
Read Romans 6:3–5.
The Word of the Lord.

All: Thanks be to God.

Go Forth!

Leader: Let us go forth this week to remember and celebrate Jesus' great love for us.

All: Thanks be to God.

 Sing "Christ Is Light"

Christ is light, in him there is no darkness.
Come to him and he will give you light.

Text: Based on 1 John 1:5. Text and music by Jack Miffleton. © 1984, OCP.
All rights reserved.

FAMILY+FAITH
LIVING AND LEARNING TOGETHER

TALKING ABOUT HOLY WEEK >>>

Holy Week is the holiest week of the Church year. It begins on Palm Sunday and continues until Evening Prayer on Easter Sunday. The Triduum or "three days" mark the most sacred time of Holy Week. It begins at sundown on Holy Thursday and ends at sundown on Easter Sunday. During these three days the whole Church fasts and prays with anticipation and hope. Christ's Resurrection is celebrated in a most solemn way during the Easter Vigil. During this long and beautiful service, Catholics recall the history of our salvation, welcome new members to the Church, and celebrate Christ's Resurrection.

God's Word

 Read **1 Corinthians 11:23b-26**, to see Saint Paul's description of the breaking of the bread at the Last Supper.

HELPING YOUR CHILD UNDERSTAND >>>
Holy Week

• Most children this age see this week as a serious one and will be open to celebrating its sacredness.

• Ordinarily at this age the Cross or crucifix is an important symbol for children.

• Children at this age will usually enjoy role-playing or acting out the stories of the Passion. Encourage them to do this with respect.

CATHOLIC FAMILY CUSTOMS >>>
The Cross

This week's lesson teaches about the importance of the cross as a means of salvation. It makes the point that each person does difficult things, or "carries a cross" at some point.

• Reinforce this idea when your child has a difficult task to face, such as giving up a treat or tolerating a medical procedure.

• Honor the crosses and crucifixes in your home by making sure to dust and clean them.

FAMILY PRAYER >>>

Lord God, Savior of the world, by your Cross and Resurrection you have set us free. We give you thanks and praise. Amen.

For a multimedia glossary of Catholic Faith Words, Sunday readings, seasonal and Saint resources, and chapter activities go to **aliveinchrist.osv.com**.

Holy, Holy, Holy

 Let Us Pray

Leader: Lord, God, send your Holy Spirit to guide us to right and loving actions. Through Christ, our Lord,

"Make known to me your ways, LORD;
    teach me your paths." **Psalm 25:4**

All: Amen.

 God's Word

Do you know that just a little yeast puffs up bread to make it high and big? Get rid of the yeast. Make yourselves like bread without yeast; Christ our Passover has been sacrificed. Let us celebrate the feast not with the old yeast of dishonesty and wickedness but with the new unleavened bread of honesty and goodness. **Based on 1 Corinthians 5:6-8**

? What Do You Wonder?

- What can hide God's presence in our lives?

- Why is being honest and truthful important?

The Holiest Day

On Easter day, the holiest day of the Church year, the Church celebrates Jesus being raised from the dead. It celebrates the everlasting life that is yours because of Jesus' Death and Resurrection. Every Sunday we celebrate a "little Easter" because that is the day Jesus rose from the dead.

A Holy People

To be holy means to be like God. God made all people to be like himself. He wants everyone to be holy. By his Death, Jesus made people holy, again. Through the waters of Baptism, Christians share in the life and holiness Jesus won for them.

At Easter Mass the assembly renews the promises made when they were baptized. The priest walks throughout the church and sprinkles everyone with the holy water that was blessed at the Easter Vigil.

➤ Where is the holy water in your parish church? When do you use it?

Easter

- During Easter, the whole Church celebrates the Resurrection of the Lord with Alleluias.

- The priest wears white vestments.

- The Church celebrates for fifty days.

Underline how Jesus made people holy again.

Easter celebrates the Resurrection of our Lord Jesus Christ.

Living Water

During the Easter season, the assembly gathered is sprinkled with holy water. This is a reminder of the importance of Baptism. Through Baptism, you share in the new life of Jesus who is risen forever.

➜ **Name some people you know who live holy lives.**

Activity

Present an Easter Play Together with your classmates, write a short play about the events of the first Easter morning. Describe your characters, costumes, props, and setting in the space below. Your class might like to present this as a play for a group of younger children.

Characters: _____

_____

Costumes and props: _____

_____

Setting: _____

_____

Celebrate Easter

 ## Let Us Pray

Gather and begin with the Sign of the Cross.

Leader: Light and peace in Jesus Christ our Lord, Alleluia.

All: Thanks be to God, Alleluia.

Leader: Let us pray.

Bow your heads as the leader prays.

All: Amen.

Sprinkling Rite

Leader: With joy you will draw water
from the fountains of salvation.   Isaiah 12:3

All: This is the day the LORD has made;
let us rejoice in it and be glad.   Psalm 118:24

As the leader sprinkles you with holy water, make the
Sign of the Cross and recall that you are a child of God.

Listen to God's Word

Reader: A reading from the holy Gospel according to Luke.
Read Luke 24:1–12.
The Gospel of the Lord.

All: Praise to you, Lord Jesus Christ.

Prayer of the Faithful

Leader: Let us pray. Jesus, you were raised from the dead so that we might live as a holy people. Listen to our loving prayers.

Respond to each prayer with these words.

All: Lord, hear our prayer.

Leader: At the Savior's command, we dare to say:

All: Our Father…

Go Forth!

Leader: Let us go to live as holy people who belong to the Risen Jesus, Alleluia, Alleluia.

All: Thanks be to God, Alleluia, Alleluia.

 Sing "This Day Was Made by the Lord"
This day was made by the Lord,
let us rejoice, let us be glad.
This day was made by the Lord,
let us rejoice in salvation!

Text: Based on Psalm 118. Text and music © 1988, 1989, Christopher Walker.
Published by OCP. All rights reserved.

FAMILY+FAITH
LIVING AND LEARNING TOGETHER

TALKING ABOUT EASTER >>>

Like Christmas, Easter is a time for family. In many areas of the country, the freshness of the earth and the spring flowers revitalize our hearts and spirits. Often we begin visiting friends and family after what seems like months of isolation during the winter.

The Feast of Easter is followed by a vibrant season of joy that continues for fifty days. All of the liturgies are uplifting, The priest wears white vestments. During the Sunday liturgies we are sprinkled with holy water to remind us of our Baptisms.

God's Word

 Read **1 Corinthians 5:6-8**, to see how Paul uses the analogy of yeast as corruption and unleavened bread as that which is without the presence of corruption.

HELPING YOUR CHILD UNDERSTAND >>>
Easter

- Most children this age are fascinated and curious about the fact of Jesus' Resurrection and what he might have looked like.

- Usually children this age have a sense of the feelings of the people who are mentioned in the post-Resurrection Gospel passages.

- For the most part, children this age can engage the post-Resurrection passages through role playing and by guided meditation.

FEASTS OF THE SEASON >>>
Ascension Thursday

Besides Easter and Pentecost the other major feast of the Easter season is Ascension Thursday, which occurs forty days after Easter and ten days before Pentecost. It celebrates Jesus' rising to go to his Father in Heaven.

FAMILY PRAYER >>>

 During the Easter Season share the following ritual at meal times.

Leader: Christ is our light!
All: Christ is our light, Alleluia.
Leader: All of the earth rejoices, because Jesus is risen from the dead! He has shown that he is God! Because of his sacrifice, we are free of the chains of death. Our lives have gained meaning because of our Redeemer. Christ is our light!
All: Alleluia, Alleluia.
Amen.

For a multimedia glossary of Catholic Faith Words, Sunday readings, seasonal and Saint resources, and chapter activities go to **aliveinchrist.osv.com**.

Pentecost

♥ Let Us Pray

Leader: Holy Spirit of the living God, send down your
power so we may bring the Good News to others.

"Send forth your spirit, they are created
and you renew the face of the earth."
Psalm 104:30

All: We ask this in the name of the Lord Jesus. Amen.

📖 God's Word

"It shall come to pass
I will pour out my spirit upon all flesh.
Your sons and daughters will prophesy,
your old men will dream dreams,
your young men will see visions.
Even upon your male and female servants,
in those days, I will pour out my spirit." Joel 3:1-2

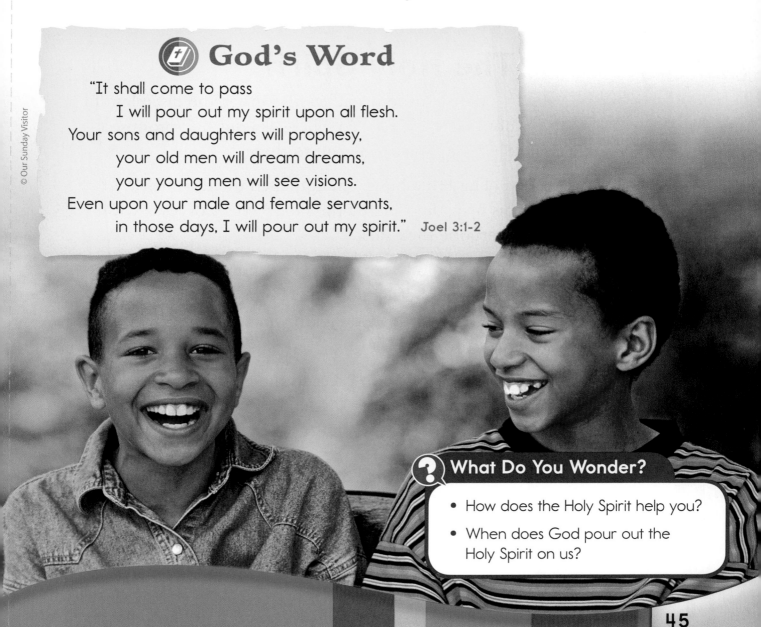

? What Do You Wonder?

- How does the Holy Spirit help you?
- When does God pour out the Holy Spirit on us?

The Holy Spirit

After Jesus returned to his Father, the disciples did not know what to do. Then, as Jesus had promised, the Holy Spirit was sent to them.

The Holy Spirit strengthened the disciples. With his help, they shared the Good News of Jesus with everyone they met.

The Good News that Jesus shared was that everyone is welcome in his Father's Kingdom. Jesus also taught that God's Kingdom is one of peace, justice, and love.

The Holy Spirit gives us the power to share the Good News of God's Kingdom with every person that we meet. On Pentecost, we pray that the Holy Spirit comes to us.

Pentecost

- The Church celebrates Pentecost fifty days after Easter.

- Pentecost celebrates the coming of the Holy Spirit upon Jesus' first disciples.

- The priest wears red vestments on Pentecost.

Underline the Good News that Jesus shared.

The Power of the Holy Spirit

The Feast of Pentecost celebrates the gift of the Holy Spirit to all of Christ's followers. With the Holy Spirit's guidance and strength, you can follow Christ and work to help build God's Kingdom of justice, love, and peace.

➤ **What are some ways that young people can show others how to follow Christ?**

Activity

Signs of Peace What are some signs of peace and justice in your parish, your school, and your country? With a partner, make a list of some of these signs. Draw a circle around one thing you can do to spread peace and love.

_____

_____

_____

_____

_____

_____

_____

Celebrate the Holy Spirit

Today you will pray a celebration of the Word. You will listen and think about God's Word. You will pray prayers of reverence by kneeling and bowing before the Bible.

 Let Us Pray

Gather and begin with the Sign of the Cross.

Leader: Light and peace in Jesus Christ our Lord, Alleluia.

All: Thanks be to God, Alleluia.

Leader: Let us pray.

Bow your heads as the leader prays.

All: Amen.

Listen to God's Word

Leader: Come, Holy Spirit, fill the hearts of your faithful.

All: And kindle in them the fire of your love.

Kneel as the Bible is carried to the prayer table. When the Bible is placed on its stand, take turns respectfully bowing in front of it.

Leader: A reading from the Acts of the Apostles.
Read Acts 2:1–11.
The Word of the Lord.

All: Thanks be to God.

Prayer of the Faithful

Leader: Let us pray. God the Holy Spirit, you fill us with your power and strength. Hear the prayers that we bring to you now.

Respond to each prayer with these words.

All: Hear our prayer, O Lord.

Leader: Let us offer praise to the Holy Trinity.

All: Glory be to the Father…

Go Forth!

Leader: Let us go forth this week to share God's Word with everyone we meet.

All: Thanks be to God.

 Sing "Alle, Alle, Alleluia"

Alle, alle, alleluia,
alle, alle, alleluia.
Alle, alle, alleluia.
Alle, alle, alle, alleluia.

FAMILY + FAITH
LIVING AND LEARNING TOGETHER

TALKING ABOUT PENTECOST >>>

The Feast of Pentecost celebrates the coming of the Holy Spirit upon the Apostles and the beginning of the early Church. Pentecost, which occurs fifty days after Easter, marks the end of the Easter season. On Pentecost, the sanctuary colors and priest's vestments are red, symbolizing the fire of Pentecost and the empowerment of the Holy Spirit. In the Scripture readings, the liturgical music, and the gestures of the assembly, the Church celebrates God's empowering activity through the gifts of the Holy Spirit.

God's Word

 Read **Joel 3:1-2**, a reading that describes what will happen when God sends his Spirit.

HELPING YOUR CHILD UNDERSTAND >>>
Pentecost

- At this age, children can quickly grasp the change in the Apostles' behavior when the Holy Spirit came upon them.

- Normally at this age children need help understanding that a mystery is something we can know, but not completely understand.

- At this age, children usually relate well to the image of the Holy Spirit as a guide and source of empowerment.

FEASTS OF THE SEASON >>>
Feast of Saint Aloysius Gonzaga
June 21

Aloysius was a spiritual young man. He became a Jesuit at 18 and died when he was 23. During that short period, he used his gifts to minister to the sick.

FAMILY PRAYER >>>

 Use the following prayer at mealtime or as an evening prayer during Pentecost week:

Come, Holy Spirit, fill the hearts of your faithful. Kindle in them the fire of your love. Send forth your Spirit, and they shall be created. And you shall renew the face of the earth. Lord, by the light of the Holy Spirit you have taught the hearts of your faithful. Help us relish what is right and rejoice in your consolation. We ask this through Christ our Lord. Amen.

 For a multimedia glossary of Catholic Faith Words, Sunday readings, seasonal and Saint resources, and chapter activities go to **aliveinchrist.osv.com**.

Revelation

Our Catholic Tradition

- Creation is all things that exist, made by God from nothing. You are part of God's plan. (CCC, 315, 317)

- We can discover God's plan in his Word—Sacred Scripture and Sacred Tradition. (CCC, 289)

- Our families show us God's love and help us know his plan for us. (CCC, 2203)

- Scripture and Tradition also tell us about God's plan for his Church, the People of God. (CCC, 781)

What are some of the ways that God shows himself to us?

The Creator's Work

 Let Us Pray

Leader: God, we praise you for your beautiful creation!

"Let them all praise the LORD's name;
for he commanded and they were
created." **Psalm 148:5**

All: We thank you God for the gifts of this world. Help
us to be responsible and respectful to all you have
given us. Amen.

 God's Word

You formed me. You made me in my mother's
womb. I praise you, because I am wonderfully made.
Wonderful is everything you have made. You knew
everything about me; even my bones you could
see. **Based on Psalm 139:13–15**

? What Do You Wonder?

- If God made all people, why are we
so different?
- Is everything that God made good?

The Creation of the World

How was everything in creation made?

God is the Creator of all things. Everything he made has a purpose and a plan. Do you remember the story of creation from the Bible?

God's Word

The Creation of the World

On the first day, God made light. He separated the light from the darkness and called them day and night.

On the second day, God separated the sky from the water below.

On the third day, God separated the land from the water. He made plants and trees.

On the fourth day, God made the moon, the sun, and the stars and put them in the sky.

On the fifth day, God made fish and birds.

On the sixth day, God made land animals.

Then God made man and woman in his image and likeness. He blessed them and put them in charge of everything he had created. And God saw that his creation was good.

On the seventh day, God rested. Based on Genesis 1:1—2:3

Learning about God

In the Bible, we learn that God alone created the universe and all forms of life. God used his power to create everything that exists. You can learn about God through his **creation**. Only God can create something where nothing existed before.

Because God is good, everything that he creates is good. In the creation story, God is shown to us as the powerful Creator who sees the goodness of all that he has made. God wants all parts of creation to work together.

© Our Sunday Visitor

Think In the green circle below draw or write about your favorite thing in God's creation.

Share Talk about God's creation with your group.

Hedchog

The Beauty of Creation

What is the purpose of God's creation?

The **Holy Trinity**—God the Father, God the Son, and God the Holy Spirit—worked as one to create the world. The Holy Trinity continues to care for and support creation. Everything God created is good and can tell you something about the love of the Trinity. You can come to know God through the beauty of creation. You can learn the truth of his goodness.

Everything in God's creation has a purpose. God wants all parts of his creation to live together in harmony and peace.

God's creation includes whales and hummingbirds, lightning and wind, sunshine and rain, and people of every color. These differences make God's world more beautiful and teach us about his greatness.

➜ What are some things you see every day that are part of God's creation?

Underline the things you can learn from God's creation.

The Image of God

God created humans in his own image and likeness and asked them to care for all creation. God wants you to live in his friendship and to be happy with him. You have a responsibility to show respect and love for God's creation. You are made in the **image of God**.

There is also sin in the world, and because of this, God's creation sometimes gets out of balance. God relies on humans to help bring back the harmony and peacefulness that he put into his creation.

Responsible to One Another

Your most important responsibility in caring for creation is to the human community. Humans are the most blessed of all God's creatures. God wants you to show respect and love for all people because he created us in his own image. In God's community of love, everyone is your brother or sister. In your unity, you can be a sign of God's goodness and love.

Catholic Faith Words

Holy Trinity the one God in three Divine Persons— God the Father, God the Son, and God the Holy Spirit

image of God the likeness of God that is in all human beings because we are created by him

Connect Your Faith

Show Your Uniqueness Work in groups of four. Next to each fingerprint, write one way that each of you are similar and one way that you are different from one another.

 We are similar because _____

_____.

 We are different because _____

_____.

Our Catholic Life

How can you show you care for all of God's creation?

God put everything we need here on Earth. The Earth gives us food. It also supplies us with materials for our clothing and our homes. God gave us all of creation to use and enjoy. When we show care for God's creation we are showing respect for other people and for the Earth.

Place a check mark next to the things you do already. Place an X next to one thing you can try to do this week.

Enjoy and Care for Creation

Enjoy Creation

- ✓ Give the flowers from the Earth as gifts.
- ✓ Use fruits and vegetables for food.
- ✓ Play sports on the grass or watch beautiful sunsets.

Care for Creation

- ✓ Respect other people and care for animals. X
- ✓ Respect the Earth by putting trash in its proper place and recyclable items in recycle bins.
- ✓ Make a commitment not to waste food or things you use every day.

People of Faith

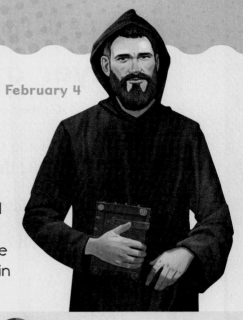

Saint Rabanus Maurus, 780–856

February 4

Saint Rabanus Maurus was a German monk and teacher. He lived a very long time ago and was one of the smartest men of his time. He studied many different things and opened a special school to help other people learn, too. He wrote many books. One was about the whole universe. Another book helped people figure out the date for Easter. Saint Rabanus wanted us to know God better by learning about the things God created. You can see some of his books in the Vatican library.

Discuss: How can you know God better by learning about the things God created?

Learn more about Saint Rabanus at **aliveinchrist.osv.com**

Live Your Faith

Make a Garden One of the best places to use and enjoy God's creation is in a garden. Imagine that you are planting a garden of your own. Write down your plans.

Things I need to start: _Seeds, shovels, soil, water._

What I'm going to plant: _I would plant vegstables and friut._

I'll care for this garden by: _Watering it every day and protecting it from indects._

How is caring for creation a way to honor God?
Because its gods creation.

♥ Let Us Pray

Prayer of Praise

Gather and begin with the Sign of the Cross.

Leader: Loving God, help us appreciate the marvelous gift of this world that you have created.

All: We thank you, God, for the gift of creation.

Leader: You made each of us wonderfully special.

All: We thank you, God, for the gift of creation.

Leader: Dear God, help us love your creation.

All: Amen.

Leader: Let us pray.

Bow your heads as the leader prays.

All: Amen.

 Sing "And It Was Good"
And it was good, good, very, very good,
and it was good, good, very, very good,
and it was good, good, very, very good,
it was very, very, very good.
Text and music: Jack Miffleton. © 1990,
OCP. All rights reserved.

FAMILY+FAITH
LIVING AND LEARNING TOGETHER

YOUR CHILD LEARNED >>>

This chapter explains how the Holy Trinity—God the Father, God the Son, and God the Holy Spirit—worked as one to create the world.

God's Word

 Read **Psalm 139:13–15** to find out how each one of us is special to God.

Catholics Believe

- God created everything. All creation shows God's goodness.
- God created humans in his image and likeness with a unique role in his creation.

To learn more, go to the *Catechism of the Catholic Church* #339, 358 at **usccb.org**.

People of Faith

This week your child met Saint Rabanus Maurus, a German monk and prototype scientist. He understood that we know God better when we learn about the things God created.

CHILDREN AT THIS AGE >>>

How They Understand Creation Third-graders enjoy being outside and are often very interested in science and nature. They understand cause and effect and are usually very curious about how things work. This is an excellent age for appreciating God's thoughtful and marvelous design and our responsibility in caring for creation.

CONSIDER THIS >>>

How much does an artist reveal about himself in his work?

Whether it is Michelangelo or your third grader, what a person creates is an extension of him or herself. Human beings are God's creation. "God's image is not a static picture stamped on our souls. God's image is a dynamic source of inner spiritual energy drawing our minds and hearts toward truth and love, and to God himself, the source of all truth and love" (*USCCA, p. 67*).

LET'S TALK >>>

- Ask your child to name some signs of God's goodness that he or she sees around them.
- Talk about the different ways you can care for God's creation as a family.

LET'S PRAY >>>

 Dear God, Saint Rabanus Maurus said we know you better when we learn about the things you created. We thank you for creating the plants and animals and each one of us. Amen.

 For a multimedia glossary of Catholic Faith Words, Sunday readings, seasonal and Saint resources, and chapter activities go to **aliveinchrist.osv.com**.

Chapter 1 Review

A **Work with Words** Fill in the circle beside the correct answer.

1. To _____ means to make something from nothing.
   ○ pray   ○ love   ○ create

2. God has given all people _____ to care for creation.
   ○ responsibility   ○ money   ○ permission

3. The one God in three Divine Persons is called the _____.
   ○ Holy Church   ○ Holy Spirit   ○ Holy Trinity

4. All creation is _____.
   ○ good   ○ bad   ○ old

5. Only _____ are created in the image of God.
   ○ animals   ○ birds   ○ humans

B **Check Understanding** Write a brief response to each question.

6. What did God create? _____

7. Who can make something from nothing?

   _____

8. How can you show that you care for creation?

   _____

9. What causes God's creation to be out of balance?

   _____

10. Who can help bring creation back into harmony?

   _____

© Our Sunday Visitor

Go to **aliveinchrist.osv.com** for an interactive review.

The Church Gathered

♡ Let Us Pray

Leader: Lord, we want to live in your presence.

"Blessed are those who dwell in your house!
They never cease to praise you." Psalm 84:5

All: Make us your house, O God. We are your people
gathered in Jesus' name. Open our hearts to the
Holy Spirit who makes us one. Amen.

📖 God's Word

"I pray not only for them, but also for those
who will believe in me through their word." I pray
that everyone who believes in me may be one
like I am one with you Father, so that the world
will believe you sent me. Based on John 17:20–23

❓ What Do You Wonder?

- How can we be one with people
all over the world?

- How can you spread the Good
News of Jesus?

Serving the Community

Where do you learn about God?

We live in communities. Life together gives us opportunities to serve one another. Here is a story about a Saint who helped his community.

Saint André Bessette

Saint André belonged to the Order of the Holy Cross. His parents died when he was young, so he did not have much schooling. The job he could do best was answering the door at a Catholic college in Canada.

Many people visited the college looking for help. Brother André helped them get what they needed. Some of the people were sick. He prayed with them and invited them to pray to Saint Joseph. Some of the people he prayed with were cured. Brother André said that God had cured them.

So many people visited Brother André to ask for his prayers that the college had to build a separate building for all of the visitors! After helping at the college, he would go out into Montreal to find more people to help. Brother André spread God's love through his life, work, and prayer.

➤ **How do you serve the communities to which you belong?**

Underline the ways that Brother André helped his community.

The early Christians gathered in house churches, catacombs, and other hidden spots.

God Teaches You

The **Bible** is the Word of God written in human words. The Bible story below tells us how the first followers of Jesus prayed, lived, and worked.

© Our Sunday Visitor

 God's Word

Helping One Another

After the Holy Spirit came, Jesus' followers met often to learn from the Apostles, to break bread together, and to pray. Some members of the group sold what they had and gave the money to help the others. Many early Christians shared their belongings with those who were in need. These followers of Jesus were very happy, and new members joined every day. Based on Acts 2:42–47

Catholic Faith Words

Bible the Word of God written in human words. The Bible is the holy book of the Church.

Share Your Faith

Think Write about a time when you've had trouble sharing with a friend or family member.

_____

_____

Share With a partner, talk about how it can sometimes be difficult to share.

God's People

Why is being part of the Church community so important?

Underline the way that being part of a community can help you.

The early Christians learned about God from Jesus and from his Apostles. God wants all people to love one another and work together like the early Christians did.

When people come together for a shared purpose, the group they form is called a community. God created you to be part of a community. A community can help you learn things about God that you might never know if you were learning on your own.

You feel God's love and share his life in the Church. The **Church** is the community of all baptized people who believe in God and follow Jesus. The word *Church* is often used for the Catholic Church because we trace our origins back to the Apostles. Jesus showed all people his Father's love, and he sent the Holy Spirit to guide the Church.

© Our Sunday Visitor

The Church community helps us learn more about God and grow in our faith.

Gathered in Jesus' Name

The word *church* comes from two different words. One word means "a community called together." The other word means "belonging to the Lord." These meanings tell you that the Church is different from other communities. The Church is the People of God. Through Baptism, God calls you to be part of this special community gathered in Jesus' name.

As a member of the Catholic Church, you have some important work to do. Church members gather together to honor and worship God and to help others. We listen to the teachings of the Church, which came from the Apostles and have been passed down to us by the bishops through **Sacred Tradition**. The Church helps us understand the Bible and the message of Jesus. She teaches us about God and his love.

Catholic Faith Words

Church the community of all baptized people who believe in God and follow Jesus. The word is often used for the Catholic Church because we trace our origins back to the Apostles.

Sacred Tradition God's Word handed down verbally through the Apostles and bishops

Connect Your Faith

God's Work Draw one way some people in your parish honor God and help others.

Our Catholic Life

Who is called to serve the Church?

Members of the Church are called together to do God's work on Earth. Each person has a special role in the Church community. You are not too young to help your Church community. Many parishes have projects that people your age can work on. Some projects go on all year. Other projects may be finished in a shorter time.

You can also serve God and the Church by living out the Good News of Jesus. You can do this in many ways.

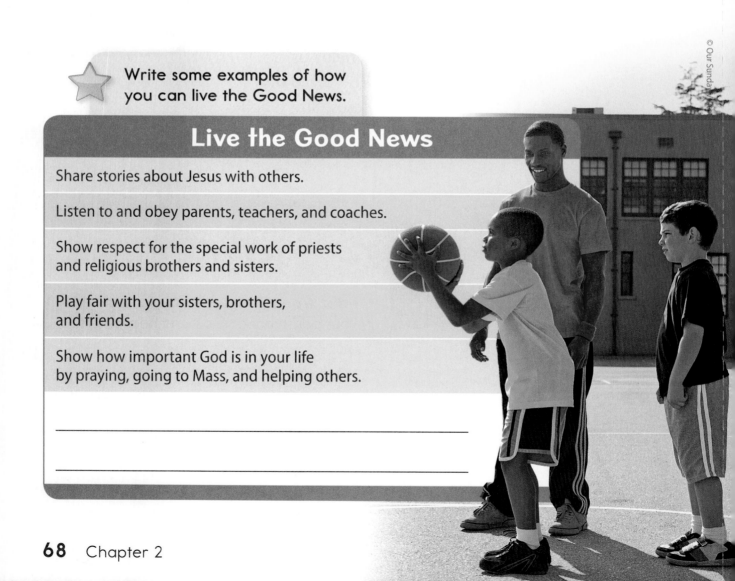

⭐ Write some examples of how you can live the Good News.

Live the Good News

Share stories about Jesus with others.

Listen to and obey parents, teachers, and coaches.

Show respect for the special work of priests and religious brothers and sisters.

Play fair with your sisters, brothers, and friends.

Show how important God is in your life by praying, going to Mass, and helping others.

_____

_____

People of Faith

Saint Francis of Assisi, 1182–1226   October 4

Saint Francis was the son of a man who sold beautiful cloth. His father wanted Francis to work with him, but Francis wanted to tell people about Jesus. One day while he was praying, Jesus asked him to rebuild the Church. Francis knew that God was calling him to do this special work. Soon other people came to help Francis. He preached the Good News of Jesus and helped make the Church more holy. He helped people to see the beauty of the world by living a simple life and showing kindness to all of God's creatures.

Discuss: How can you be kind to all of God's creatures?

 Learn more about Saint Francis at **aliveinchrist.osv.com**

Live Your Faith

Write a Story List four ways that people do God's work every day. Choose one way from the list and write about a person your age who does this.

1. _____

2. _____

3. _____

4. _____

_____

_____

_____

_____

_____

 Let Us Pray

Prayer of Thanksgiving

Gather and begin with the Sign of the Cross.

Leader: Jesus, you call us in so many ways. We thank you now for being part of the Catholic Church.

Reader 1: The Church is the People of God

Reader 2: gathered in the name of Jesus.

All: Thank you for calling us to be a part of your Church.

Reader 3: The Church helps us to understand the Bible

Reader 4: and to share the message and love of Jesus.

All: Thank you for calling us to be a part of your Church.

Reader 5: The Church helps us to honor God the Father

Reader 6: and to grow closer to Jesus.

All: Thank you for calling us to be a part of your Church.

Leader: Let us pray.

Bow your heads as the leader continues to pray.

Sing "We Come Today"

FAMILY+FAITH
LIVING AND LEARNING TOGETHER

YOUR CHILD LEARNED >>>

This chapter explains how the Church community works together to act in Jesus' name.

God's Word

 Read **John 17:20–23** and talk about the ways each of you can be one with God.

Catholics Believe

- The Bible is the Word of God written in human words.
- The Church is the community of all baptized people who believe in God and follow Jesus.

To learn more, go to the *Catechism of the Catholic Church* #781, 782 at **usccb.org**.

People of Faith

This week, your child met Saint Francis of Assisi, who helped bring about a renewal of Church through his simple way of life.

CHILDREN AT THIS AGE >>>

How They Understand the Church Community Third grade is an age when the social group often becomes important to children. They want to know that they belong and have friends. This is the perfect age to talk with your child about the Church as our community of faith. It's especially important that they have time to spend with peers at church and are able to form friendships in their parish community.

CONSIDER THIS >>>

When someone looks at you do they see Christ in you?

Have you ever asked yourself this? It may seem like an odd question. Yet, as baptized people we believe that God has invited us into his Divine life. "Only Jesus can transform us into himself. Our inner receptivity [our openness] is critical. To receive love, we need to be open to it." Offering ourselves at Mass together with the gifts of bread and wine is the best way to continuously give Christ the opportunity to transform us. "Then in Christ we become bread for the world's bodily and spiritual hungers" (*USCCA*, p. 227).

LET'S TALK >>>

- As a family, talk about ways that you could live a more simple life.
- Talk about the different times you gather as a Church community.

LET'S PRAY >>>

 Saint Francis, pray for us that we may work together to build the Church. Amen.

 For a multimedia glossary of Catholic Faith Words, Sunday readings, seasonal and Saint resources, and chapter activities go to **aliveinchrist.osv.com**.

Chapter 2 Review

A **Work with Words** Complete the following statements.

Word Bank

Church

Good News

community

People of God

Bible

1. One way to serve God and the Church is by living out the _____ of Jesus Christ.

2. A _____ is a group of people who come together for a shared purpose.

3. The _____ is the community of all baptized people who believe in God and follow Jesus.

4. The _____ is the Word of God written in human words.

5. A name for the Church community is _____.

B **Check Understanding** Match each description in Column A with the correct term in Column B.

Column A	Column B
6. Was sent to guide the Church	Sacred Tradition
7. Means "belonging to the Lord"	the Holy Spirit
8. Showing respect for others is one way to do this	love
9. God's Word handed down verbally through the Apostles and bishops	Church
10. God wants people to show each other this	serve God

Go to **aliveinchrist.osv.com** for an interactive review.

Families Teach Love

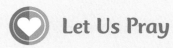 **Let Us Pray**

Leader: God, our Father, help us to live as your people.

"How good and how pleasant it is,
when brothers dwell together as one!"   Psalm 133:1

All: God, you give us our families to teach us about you.
Help us to listen, learn, and follow your ways. Amen.

God's Word

Jesus' Mother and others from his family came to see him but could not get near him because of the crowd. Someone told him, "Your family is outside and they want to see you." Jesus said, "My mother and my brothers are those who hear the word of God and act on it."   Based on Luke 8:19–21

? What Do You Wonder?

- How are you a part of Jesus' family?

- Does God really care if you obey your parents?

A Model for Our Families

What does Mary teach us about being part of a family?

Catholic Faith Words

Visitation the name of Mary's visit to Elizabeth before Jesus was born

Mary the Mother of Jesus, the Mother of God. She is also called "Our Lady" because she is our Mother and the Mother of the Church.

In our families, we learn to care about and respect each other. We learn how important it is to listen to each other and be there when someone needs help. We share our lives. This story from the Bible, called the **Visitation**, tells us about a visit between **Mary** and her cousin Elizabeth.

 **God's Word**

Mary Visits Elizabeth

Mary's cousin, Elizabeth, was happy and surprised when Mary visited. Filled with the Holy Spirit, Elizabeth said to Mary,

"Most blessed are you among women, and blessed is the fruit of your womb. And how does this happen to me, that the mother of my Lord should come to me?"

Elizabeth's greeting made Mary happy. She answered, "My soul proclaims the greatness of the Lord; my spirit rejoices in God my savior."

Based on Luke 1:39–47

The Greatest Mother

Like the Angel Gabriel who said to Mary, "Hail, favored one! The Lord is with you," Elizabeth knew how special Mary was (Luke 1:28). As Catholics, we have always recognized Mary as a special member of God's family and the greatest Saint. She perfectly lived God's plan for her. We honor Mary as the Mother of God and our Mother. One way we do this is when we pray the Hail Mary.

➡ **How can we honor Mary?**

Complete the prayer and then pray it together as a group

The Hail Mary

Hail, Mary, full of _____,

the Lord is with thee.

_____ art thou among women

and blessed is the fruit of thy womb, _____.

Holy Mary, _____ of God,

pray for us sinners, now and at the hour of our death. Amen.

Share Your Faith

Think Write one way your family members love and care for one another.

_____

_____

_____

Share with a partner.

The Church of the Home

How can our families help to show us God's love?

Catholic Faith Words

domestic Church a name for the Catholic family, because it is the community of Christians in the home. God made the family to be the first place we learn about loving others and following Christ.

In the story of the Visitation, Mary and Elizabeth helped us see how family members' actions show love. Your family members may show their love in actions, in words, or both.

You first learn about God's love for you from your family. Your family also teaches you how to love God and others.

You learn the basics of healthy living from your family. They teach you important safety rules. You may learn how to care for pets or do other chores.

Your family helps you learn prayers, such as the blessing before meals, the Lord's Prayer, and the Hail Mary. Your family introduces you to the Catholic Church. If you are baptized, you are already a member of this special family of God. The Church builds on what you have learned in your home. For this reason, the family is called the "**domestic Church**," or the Church of the home.

Communities of Love

The Church of the home can be a special sign that shows others how the three Persons of the Holy Trinity love one another. Your family is a sign of this love when you live together in faith, hope, and love.

God shares his authority with parents. He invites them to love and care for you just as he does. God wants you to respect your parents and others who care for you. This includes teachers and community officials. Their authority comes from God, too.

God Loves Everyone

Sometimes members of families may be busy or tired. They may let you down. They are still loved by God, just as you are. It is important to treat the members of your family with love and respect and to pray for them.

Underline how your family is a sign of the love of the Holy Trinity.

Connect Your Faith

Make a Caring Chart What words and actions show love in each of these situations? Write your ideas in each column.

The Visitation	My Family Life
_____	_____
_____	_____
_____	_____
_____	_____

Our Catholic Life

How do you show respect for God and others?

God cares for you more than anyone else can. He showed that he cares about you by giving you life. God also gave you a family and the Church to guide you. He wants you to treat your family members with respect because they are a gift.

Write one more way you can show respect for God and one more way you can show respect for others.

Respect

Respect for God	Respect for Others
You can show respect for God by • following the Ten Commandments. • teaching others about God. • taking part in Mass. • helping your Church community.	You show respect • for family members by treating them with love and care. • for your friends by taking turns and sharing your games. • for your teachers by doing your assignments and by being polite. • for your classmates by listening when they talk and by inviting them into your games.
_____	_____
_____	_____
_____	_____
_____	_____

People of Faith

Blessed Luigi Beltrame Quattrocchi, 1880–1951 and Blessed Maria Corsini, 1884–1965

November 25

Blessed Luigi and Maria were a married couple. They lived in Rome, Italy. Luigi was a lawyer. Maria was a writer and a catechist. They had four children whom they loved very much. The family had a lot of fun together, but they always made time for prayer and helping other people. During World War II, they let people who had lost their homes stay with them. They showed the love of Jesus to everyone they met. Blessed Luigi and Maria help us see how our homes and families can be a domestic Church.

Discuss: How does your family show the love of Jesus?

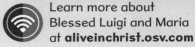

Learn more about Blessed Luigi and Maria at **aliveinchrist.osv.com**

Live Your Faith

Create a Comic Strip Draw a comic strip about a family whose members use words and actions to show that they care for one another.

 **Let Us Pray**

Prayer of Petition

Gather and begin with the Sign of the Cross.

Leader: Dear God, you give us families to love and guide us. With your help, we will try to show them our love and care.

Reader 1: When we are together,

All: Help us show love and care.

Reader 2: When family members are sad,

All: Help us show love and care.

Reader 3: When we are full of energy and ideas,

All: Help us show love and care.

Reader 4: When we are tired and grouchy,

All: Help us show love and care.

Leader: Dear God, thank you for caring families.

All: Amen.

Leader: Let us pray.

Bow your heads as the leader prays.

All: Amen.

 Sing "The Family of God"
We gather together to celebrate family.
Our Church is the Family of God.
Sharing together the blessing of Jesus,
the Family of God.
© 2010, Chet A. Chambers. Published by Our Sunday Visitor, Inc.

FAMILY+FAITH
LIVING AND LEARNING TOGETHER

YOUR CHILD LEARNED >>>

This chapter explores Mary as a model for family living and how families show love and respect and the role of the family as the domestic Church.

God's Word

 Read **Luke 8:19–21** and talk about how each of you hear God's Word and try to live by it.

Catholics Believe

- Mary is a special member of God's family and the greatest Saint.
- The family home is called the "domestic Church."

To learn more, go to the *Catechism of the Catholic Church* #1657, 1666 at **usccb.org**.

People of Faith

This week, your child met Blessed Luigi Beltrame Quattrocchi and Blessed Maria Corsini, the first married couple to be beatified together.

CHILDREN AT THIS AGE >>>

How They Understand the Family as Domestic Church
A family's professed beliefs, and especially their example, are very important and powerful forces that shape the faith of children. It's important that the two match as much as reasonably possible, because your child is now at the age when he or she can notice discrepancies between words and actions.

CONSIDER THIS >>>

How do electronic devices keep your family from being present to each other?

When we are checking emails, texting, talking on the phone, and playing games on our tablet with no boundaries, sacred family time starts to disappear. Being in the same room is not enough. Being present to one another is the first obligation and privilege of family life. "When family members pray together, engage in lifelong learning, forgive one another, [and] serve each other…they help each other live the faith and grow in faith" *(USCCA, p. 376).*

LET'S TALK >>>

- Ask your child to name someone in his or her life, other than a parent, who helps him/her live a holy life?
- Talk about the different ways you can treat the members of your family with love and respect.

LET'S PRAY >>>

 Heavenly Father, like Blessed Luigi and Blessed Maria, help us serve you and one another through a holy family life. Amen.

For a multimedia glossary of Catholic Faith Words, Sunday readings, seasonal and Saint resources, and chapter activities go to **aliveinchrist.osv.com**.

Chapter 3 Review

A **Work with Words** Complete each sentence with the correct word or words from the Word Bank.

Word Bank

domestic Church

authority

respect

love

Hail Mary

1. You can show _____ for God by following the Ten Commandments.

2. Elizabeth's words to Mary are found in the _____.

3. _____ is a name for the Catholic family and the first place we learn about God.

4. Families are a sign of God's _____.

5. The Church wants you to respect _____.

B **Check Understanding** Write the letter T if the sentence is TRUE. Write the letter F if the sentence is FALSE.

6. Mary's visit to Elizabeth is called the Holy Greeting. ☐

7. God gives parents and teachers the authority to love and care for you. ☐

8. Family members show one another care by giving gifts and money. ☐

Write responses on the lines below.

9. Why should you respect God and your family members?

_____

10. How do you show respect for your family members?

_____

Go to **aliveinchrist.osv.com** for an interactive review.

A **Work with Words**
Solve the crossword puzzle.

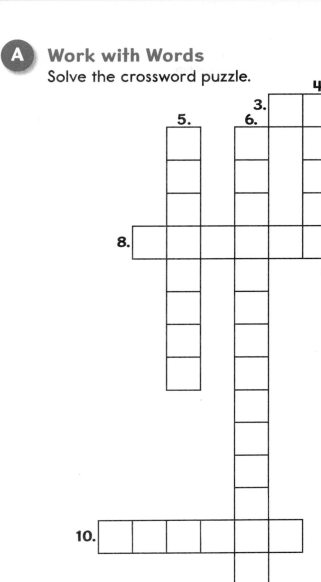

Down

1. Family members should love and
   _____ one another.

2. When Mary went to stay with
   Elizabeth.

4. Humans were created in God's
   _____.

5. The _____ Church is the
   community of Christians in
   the home.

6. A duty or job that you are
   trusted to do.

7. Community of all baptized
   people who believe in God
   and follow Jesus.

Across

3. The Word of God
   written in human words.

8. A name for the Church is the
   _____ of God.

9. God gives this to parents and
   those who care for you.

10. The Holy Trinity worked as one
    to _____ the world.

B **Check Understanding** Match each description in Column A with the correct term in Column B.

Column A   Column B

11. We call God the Father, God the Son, and God the Holy Spirit this   humans

12. The most blessed of all creatures   Holy Trinity

13. A group of people who come together for a shared purpose   good

14. All creation is this   Jesus Christ

15. The Church is gathered in his name   community

C **Make Connections** Name five ways you can show respect for God.

16. _____

_____

17. _____

_____

18. _____

_____

19. _____

_____

20. _____

_____

Name five ways you can show respect for others.

21. _____

_____

22. _____

_____

23. _____

_____

24. _____

_____

25. _____

_____

Trinity

The assembly comes together at Mass to worship the Holy Trinity.

© Our Sunday Visitor

Our Catholic Tradition

- The mystery of the Holy Trinity is the most important mystery of our faith. (CCC, 261)

- The Trinity is the one God in three Divine Persons who are united in love. (CCC, 263)

- Each of the Divine Persons of the Trinity is distinct, and they work together in love. (CCC, 267)

- We worship the Trinity when we gather for Mass and in personal prayer. (CCC, 1325, 2565)

How do we grow in love with God the Father, God the Son, and God the Holy Spirit?

The Holy Trinity

 Let Us Pray

Leader: Lord God, send the Holy Spirit to set our hearts on fire!

"The grace of the Lord Jesus Christ and the love of God and the fellowship of the holy Spirit be with all of you." **2 Corinthians 13:13**

All: God, you are so much more than our minds can ever understand. Be with us as we explore the mystery of your great love. Amen.

 God's Word

This is how we know that we remain in Jesus, and he is with us, that he has given us his Spirit. "Moreover, we have seen and testify that the Father sent his Son as savior of the world. We have come to know and to believe in the love God has for us."

Based on 1 John 4:13–14, 16

? **What Do You Wonder?**

- Who is God?
- If you cannot see God right now, how do you know he is here?

One God, Three Divine Persons

What can we learn about the Holy Trinity?

Have you ever learned something that was hard to understand? The story of Saint Patrick tells how the people of Ireland learned about the Holy Trinity.

Saint Patrick

Long ago, the people of Ireland had questions about God. As a bishop, Patrick was teaching about the three Divine Persons in one God. Someone asked, "How can you say that there is only one God when you pray to the Father, the Son, and the Holy Spirit?"

Patrick explained the mystery of the Holy Trinity by plucking a shamrock from the ground. He held it up for the people to see.

"The shamrock is one plant, but it has three leaves. The Father, Son, and Holy Spirit are not three gods. They are one God in three Divine Persons. This is a **mystery** that we accept on faith."

Catholic Faith Words

mystery a spiritual truth that is difficult to perceive or understand with our senses, but is known through faith and through signs

Incarnation the mystery that the Son of God became man to save all people

© Our Sunday Visitor

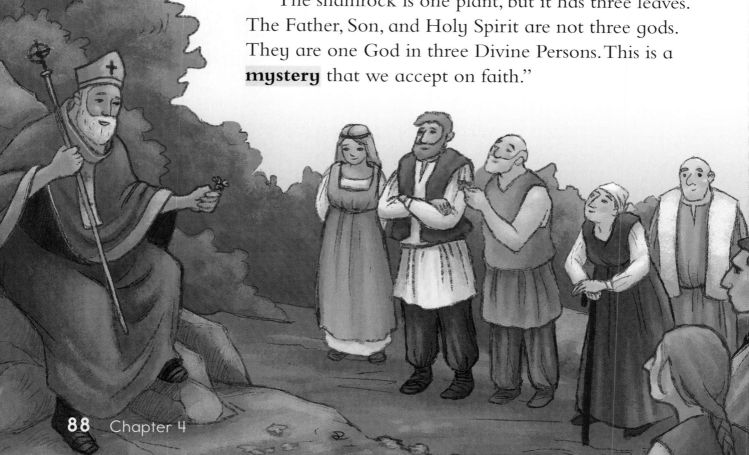

Jesus Makes the Mystery Known

Patrick helped the people understand that there is only one God. You can also learn from Jesus, who told his followers about the Father and the Holy Spirit.

 God's Word

The Father and the Spirit

One day Jesus was talking with his followers about God. Jesus told them, "No one comes to the Father except through me. If you know me, then you will also know my Father."

Jesus promised to ask the Father to send the Holy Spirit to teach and guide the people.   Based on John 14:6–7, 16–17

Along with the shamrock, a triangle or three interlocking rings are also used to explain the Holy Trinity.

Underline what Jesus said about the Father.

There are three persons in one God:

- **God the Father** Jesus called God "Father," and he taught his followers to call God "Father," too.

- **God the Son** By his actions, Jesus showed that he is God the Son, who became man to save all people. This is known as the **Incarnation**.

- **God the Holy Spirit** Jesus asked his Father to send the Holy Spirit, who is God's love and grace, to be present with us.

Share Your Faith

Think How can symbols help you understand that the Trinity is one God in three Divine Persons?

Share your answer with a partner.

Communion of Love

What is the work of the Holy Trinity?

The most important thing about the Holy Trinity is that he is a loving communion of Divine Persons joined as one in love.

The Holy Trinity is a mystery, a truth of faith that Catholics believe even though we cannot understand it completely. A mystery is a truth that only God can fully understand. But, Jesus came to help us begin to see that God the Father, God the Son, and God the Holy Spirit are a perfect communion of love. The Holy Trinity is one God in three Divine Persons.

Through God's revelation and with his help, you can understand more about a mystery like the Trinity. You can see the Trinity at work when you see love in the world. You can see the reflection of the Trinity in the Church. You will better understand the Trinity when you see God in Heaven.

Catholic Faith Words

creed a statement of the Church's beliefs

Apostles' Creed one of the Church's oldest creeds. It is a summary of Christian beliefs taught since the time of the Apostles. This creed is used in the celebration of Baptism.

Underline the most important thing about the Holy Trinity.

Honoring the Trinity

The Church remembers and honors the one God in three Divine Persons in such prayers as the Sign of the Cross and the Glory Be and in the creeds. A **creed** is a statement of the Church's beliefs. One of the oldest creeds is the **Apostles' Creed**. It is a summary of faith in the Holy Trinity. Here is how the three parts begin.

"I believe in God, the Father …

I believe in Jesus Christ …

I believe in the Holy Spirit …"

Working Together

God the Father created you. God the Son, Jesus Christ, saved you and is your brother. God the Holy Spirit is with you now, making you holy and helping you bring God's love and peace to the world. All three Persons of the Trinity work together as one God.

➡ **When can the Holy Spirit help and guide you?**

Connect Your Faith

Write a Prayer Finish each prayer in your own words.

God our Father, _____

_____

Jesus, Son of God, _____

_____

Holy Spirit, _____

_____

Our Catholic Life

Who answers your questions about the Church?

You are growing in your understanding of the Catholic faith. You probably have some questions about what you have been learning this year. It is all right to ask questions when you want to understand something better. There are people in the Church who will be glad to help you find the answers.

Finding Answers

There are many places to go to find answers to your questions about the Catholic faith. Ask your parents or guardians, your parish priest, or a religious education teacher to help you find the answers. They can probably lead you to the correct information source. Here are some places to look:

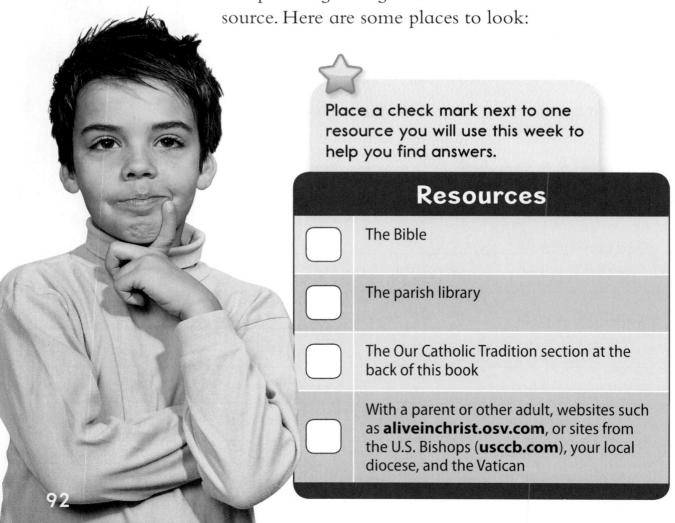

Place a check mark next to one resource you will use this week to help you find answers.

Resources

☐	The Bible
☐	The parish library
☐	The Our Catholic Tradition section at the back of this book
☐	With a parent or other adult, websites such as **aliveinchrist.osv.com**, or sites from the U.S. Bishops (**usccb.com**), your local diocese, and the Vatican

People of Faith

Saint John of Matha, 1160–1213

Febuary 8

Saint John of Matha was born in France. From the time he was a very little boy he tried to show his love for the Trinity. He obeyed his parents and studied hard. For a while he lived alone as a hermit. But he decided that God wanted him to become a priest, so he went to Paris. After he was ordained, he started a group of priests called the Order of the Most Holy Trinity or Trinitarians. They worked to free Christians who were slaves. There are still Trinitarian priests today. They honor the Trinity by working in schools and churches.

Discuss: How can you show that you love the Father, the Son, and the Holy Spirit?

Learn more about Saint John at **aliveinchrist.osv.com**

Live Your Faith

Write a Letter Who do you think can help you learn more about the Catholic faith? Draft a letter to that person and ask a question about your Catholic faith.

Dear _____,

_____

_____

_____

_____

_____

Let Us Pray

Profess Our Faith

Gather and begin with the Sign of the Cross.

Leader: Joined together as one community, we are called to one faith.

Reader: A reading from the Letter to the Ephesians.

Read Ephesians 4:1–6.

The Word of the Lord.

All: Thanks be to God.

Leader: Let us share our belief in the Trinity. Do you believe in God the Father?

All: I do.

Leader: Do you believe in Jesus Christ, his only Son?

All: I do.

Leader: Do you believe in the Holy Spirit, the Lord and giver of life?

All: I do.

Leader: This is our faith. This is the faith of the Church.

All: Amen.

 Sing "Yes, Lord, I Believe"

FAMILY+FAITH
LIVING AND LEARNING TOGETHER

YOUR CHILD LEARNED >>>

This chapter examines the mystery of the Holy Trinity and the relationship between God the Father, God the Son, and God the Holy Spirit.

God's Word

 Read **1 John 4:13–14, 16** and talk about how each of you know and believe in the Trinity.

Catholics Believe

- The Holy Trinity is one God in three Divine Persons.
- Jesus, God the Son, taught about God the Father and God the Holy Spirit.

To learn more, go to the *Catechism of the Catholic Church* #253, 237 at **usccb.org**.

People of Faith

This week, your child met Saint John of Matha, the founder of the Trinitarians. Saint John is known for his work in freeing Christian slaves in Tunis.

CHILDREN AT THIS AGE >>>

How They Understand The Trinity Because community is so important to many third-grade children, this is a perfect age to explore our understanding that God himself is a communion of Divine Persons. Your child is learning that community (and communion) between persons means mutual giving of self (especially important in parent-child and spousal relationships). This self-giving love is also evident in God's revelation of himself to us. The Trinity is a communion of three Divine Persons.

CONSIDER THIS >>>

How important is it to live what you believe?

Most people want to be seen as a person of integrity—a person who lives what he or she believes. So, we must be clear about what we believe. "The Church hears the perennial questions that each person asks at some point: 'How shall I live?' 'What values or principles shall I accept?' 'What norms shall I make my own?' 'What gives meaning to my life?' To answer questions such as these, we turn to a wise teacher. Christ is the ultimate teacher, and he continues to be heard in and through the Church today" (*USCCA, p. 330*).

LET'S TALK >>>

- Ask your child to explain how the shamrock helps us understand the Holy Trinity.
- Give examples of how the Holy Spirit has helped guide you in your life.

LET'S PRAY >>>

 Saint John, pray for us that we may honor the Trinity by serving others at work, at school, and at home. Amen.

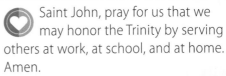 For a multimedia glossary of Catholic Faith Words, Sunday readings, seasonal and Saint resources, and chapter activities go to **aliveinchrist.osv.com**.

A **Work with Words** Complete the following statements.

1. A statement of Church beliefs is a _____.

2. The name given to the one God in three Divine Persons is the _____.

3. A spiritual truth that is hard to understand is called a _____.

4. All three Persons of the Trinity work together as one _____.

5. Saint Patrick taught about the Trinity by using a _____.

B **Check Understanding** Fill in the circle beside the correct answer.

6. The _____ describes the Son of God becoming man.
   ○ Incarnation
   ○ Mystery
   ○ Annunciation

7. Jesus called God "_____."
   ○ Trinity
   ○ Father
   ○ Sir

8. One of the Church's oldest creeds is the _____.
   ○ prayers
   ○ Scriptures
   ○ Apostles' Creed

9. The Holy Spirit helps bring love and _____ to the world.
   ○ peace
   ○ sin
   ○ riches

10. You _____ learn more about your Catholic faith from people in the Church.
    ○ can
    ○ cannot
    ○ should not

 Go to **aliveinchrist.osv.com** for an interactive review.

The Church Celebrates

 Let Us Pray

Leader: Holy Father, we celebrate your love for us. Let us look at all that you have made and say, "This is awesome!"

"Give praise with tambourines and dance,
   praise him with strings and pipes." Psalm 150:4

All: With all that you have given us God, our hearts are full of praise and we thank you. Amen.

God's Word

A very large crowd gathered to listen to Jesus. They were hungry. Jesus told the people to sit down. "Then, taking the five loaves and the two fish and looking up to heaven, he said the blessing, broke the loaves, and gave them to [his] disciples to set before the people; he also divided the two fish among them all." Everyone ate until they were full. Based on Mark 6:34–42

? What Do You Wonder?

- How do you give thanks to God?
- How does Jesus feed us today?

Special Celebrations

Why do Church members celebrate together?

© Our Sunday Visitor

Parties or meals with family and friends are great ways to celebrate important events, birthdays, and holidays. As Catholics, we celebrate special times in our faith and the life of the Church. We come together to worship God, honoring him with prayers and actions. We do this in a special way when we celebrate the **Seven Sacraments**.

Jesus taught his followers how to celebrate and thank God. He told stories and shared meals with them. His last meal with them was the most memorable one of all.

When Catholics celebrate the Mass, we remember what Jesus said and did at the **Last Supper**. We gather to give praise and thank God for the many gifts he has given us, most especially the gift of Jesus' Body and Blood, our greatest reason to celebrate.

➜ **What are some ways we celebrate and thank God?**

God's Word

The Last Supper

Jesus and his disciples were together to celebrate the Jewish feast of Passover.

Jesus blessed the bread and broke it. He gave the bread to his friends, saying, "This is my body, which will be given for you; do this in memory of me."

Jesus then took the cup of wine and said, "This cup is the new covenant in my blood, which will be shed for you."

Based on Luke 22:14–20

 Underline what Jesus did with the bread.

At Mass, the priest blesses the bread as Jesus did at the Last Supper and it becomes the Body of Christ.

 ## Share Your Faith

Think Write about your favorite special celebration that you share with your family.

_____

_____

_____

_____

_____

Share with a partner.

The Heart of Our Worship

What happens in the Mass?

You can worship God alone or with your Church parish community. Worship is a way to return the love that God shows you. You can worship God with words, silence, music, and actions.

At the celebration of the Eucharist and in the other Sacraments, Catholics worship as a community. This kind of public, community worship is called **liturgy**.

Although Catholics have many ways to pray and worship, the Eucharist, or the Mass, is the most important. In the Eucharist, the community joins with Jesus to worship God the Father through the power of the Holy Spirit. The community joins in the love of the Holy Trinity.

At Mass

At Mass, Catholics gather to hear God's Word in Scripture. We profess our faith, or say what we believe about the Holy Trinity and the Church. We usually do this by saying the **Nicene Creed**. During the Mass, we remember and celebrate what Jesus said and did with his disciples at the Last Supper.

Catholic Faith Words

liturgy the public prayer of the Church. It includes the Sacraments and forms of daily prayer.

Nicene Creed a summary of basic beliefs about God the Father, God the Son, and God the Holy Spirit and about other Church teachings. We usually say the Nicene Creed during Mass.

Every time you go to Mass, you are encouraged to receive Jesus' Body and Blood in Holy Communion. The Church requires that you do this at least once during the Easter Season.

The Church teaches that Catholics must attend Mass on Sundays, or Saturday evenings, and Holy Days of Obligation. The celebration of the Eucharist is the center of the Church's life. When you do this, you follow the Third Commandment, "Remember to keep holy the Lord's Day."

Outside of Mass, Catholics also show love and respect for Jesus in the Eucharist by visiting the **Blessed Sacrament** in church. The Body of Christ is kept in the **Tabernacle**. Jesus Christ remains truly present in the Blessed Sacrament.

➡ **How does your family keep holy the Lord's Day?**

Catholic Faith Words

Blessed Sacrament a name for the Holy Eucharist, especially the Body of Christ kept in the Tabernacle

Tabernacle the special place in the church where the Blessed Sacrament is reserved after Mass for those who are ill or for Eucharistic Adoration

Connect Your Faith

Give Praise Write a verse of joy, praise, or thanks for the gift of the Eucharist in the space below.

_____

_____

_____

_____

_____

_____

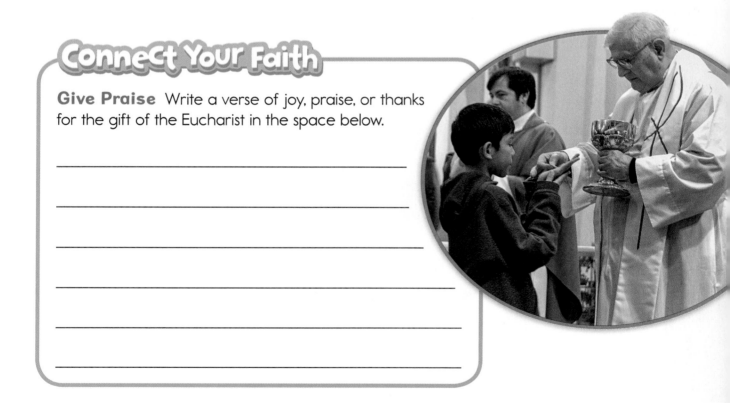

Our Catholic Life

How do you show respect at Mass?

One way to show honor and respect for God is to always act your best at Mass.

Underline one way that you have shown respect for God at Mass.

- Bow or genuflect before sitting down. When you bow, bend the upper part of your body from the waist. When you genuflect, you respectfully bend one knee and touch it to the floor.

- Sing the songs and pray the prayers.

- Listen to the priest.

- Stand in line with your hands folded when processing up to receive Holy Communion and bow slightly as the person before you is receiving.

- Stand up straight and tall, and make sure that you are a part of the celebration!

Worship Together

Members of the Church use certain actions during Mass to show respect for God. You make the Sign of the Cross and sit, stand, and kneel at certain times.

The prayers of the Church are special ways of honoring God. At Mass, you pray the Lord's Prayer and other prayers. When you pray the prayers of the Church, you join Catholics all over the world.

People of Faith

Saint Mary MacKillop, 1842–1909

August 8

Saint Mary MacKillop is the first person to become a Saint from Australia. She was a teacher. She rode horses a long way into the desert, called the Australian Outback, to teach children. She taught the children of farmers and miners. She also used to teach the native Australians, called Aborigines. When she was made a Saint, many Aborigines came to the ceremony in Italy. They wore face paint, danced traditional dances, and played special musical instruments called didgeridoos during the Mass. It was their way of showing how much they loved Saint Mary. Saint Mary loved them, too.

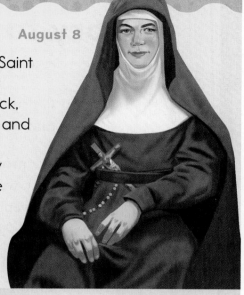

Discuss: What is your favorite part about going to Mass?

Learn more about Saint Mary MacKillop at **aliveinchrist.osv.com**

Live Your Faith

Draw Yourself Under each picture, describe what is happening. Then, draw yourself at Mass in the empty box.

_____   _____   _____

Me at Mass

Let Us Pray

Glory to God

Gather and begin with the Sign of the Cross.

All: Glory to God in the highest,
and on earth peace to people of good will.

We praise you, we bless you, we adore you, we glorify
you, we give you thanks for your great glory, Lord God,
heavenly King, O God, almighty Father.

Lord Jesus Christ,
Only Begotten Son,
Lord God, Lamb of God,
Son of the Father,
you take away the sins of the world,
have mercy on us;
you take away the sins of the world,
receive our prayer;
you are seated at the right hand of the Father,
have mercy on us.

For you alone are the Holy One,
you alone are the Lord,
you alone are the Most High,
Jesus Christ, with the Holy Spirit,
in the glory of God the Father. Amen.

 Sing "Praise the Lord"
Praise, praise the Lord.
Praise, praise the Lord.
Praise the name of the Lord God
most high.

© 2011, Banner Kidd. Published by Our Sunday Visitor, Inc.

FAMILY+FAITH
LIVING AND LEARNING TOGETHER

YOUR CHILD LEARNED >>>

This chapter explains how we worship as Catholics and the special place of the Eucharist among the Seven Sacraments.

God's Word

 Read **Mark 6:34–42** and talk about how God gives you what you need.

Catholics Believe

- The celebration of the Eucharist is the Church's most important form of worship.
- In the Eucharist, the Church remembers what Jesus said and did at the Last Supper and receives the Body and Blood of Christ.

To learn more, go to the *Catechism of the Catholic Church* #1333, 1407 at **usccb.org**.

People of Faith

This week, your child met Saint Mary MacKillop, the first Saint from Australia. Point out the continents on a map and talk about how there have been Saints from every part of the world.

CHILDREN AT THIS AGE >>>

How They Understand the Mass The Mass is the gathering of the parish community to remember and be present with Jesus Christ. At Mass, we gather to praise God and give him thanks for the many gifts he has given us, most especially the gift of Jesus' Body and Blood. This understanding of the Mass as a community celebration and the vehicle Jesus has chosen to be continually present with us is an important one to third-graders, who are developing in their understanding of community.

CONSIDER THIS >>>

Why do you teach your children to say thank-you?

Gratitude has its own rewards. It creates a loving connection to those we thank. It acknowledges that we understand the value of the gift. If we pay attention to our lives, we begin to recognize that everything is a gift from God. Our hearts fill to the point of bursting—with gratitude. We devotedly participate in Mass to say thank-you. "The Eucharistic sacrifice is offered to adore and thank God, to pray for all our needs, and to gain pardon for our sins" (*USCCA, p. 221*). As a result of our participation, our relationship with God intensifies.

LET'S TALK >>>

- Explain that the Mass is the same no matter where you go.
- Share what you find most meaningful in the Mass and then have your child do so as well.

LET'S PRAY >>>

 Dear God, Saint Mary MacKillop brought God's Word to different parts of the world. Help us to worship you with our minds, our hearts, and our bodies at Mass. Amen.

 For a multimedia glossary of Catholic Faith Words, Sunday readings, seasonal and Saint resources, and chapter activities go to **aliveinchrist.osv.com**.

Chapter 5 Review

A **Work with Words** Complete each sentence with the letter of the correct word or words from the Word Bank.

Word Bank

a. Tabernacle

b. Blessed Sacrament

c. holy

d. Passover

e. Scripture

1. At his last meal, Jesus and his friends celebrated the Jewish feast of ☐.

2. The Holy Eucharist, especially the Body of Christ kept in the Tabernacle is called the ☐.

3. At Mass, Catholics gather to hear God's Word in ☐.

4. The Third Commandment says to keep ☐ the Lord's day.

5. After Mass, the Eucharist is kept in the ☐.

B **Check Understanding** Fill in the blanks with the correct answers.

6. What is worship? _____

7. What is the most important way Catholics worship God?

   _____

8. How often and when must Catholics receive Holy Communion?

   _____

9. What is liturgy?

   _____

10. When must Catholics attend Mass?

    _____

    _____

Go to **aliveinchrist.osv.com** for an interactive review.

Pray Always

 Let Us Pray

Leader: O God, listen to our prayers. We offer you our hearts filled with love.

"Attend to the sound of my cry,
my king and my God!" Psalm 5:3

All: Jesus, you ask us to be people who pray. Help us to trust that you listen to our prayers. Amen.

 God's Word

Jesus told his disciples not to be like the people who pray loudly in public so that others can see and hear them. Jesus said to go to a private place, close the door, and pray quietly to the Father. God will hear you.

Based on Matthew 6:5–6

? What Do You Wonder?

• How does God hear the prayers of all the people in the world?

• Can you pray to God about anything that is bothering you?

Jesus Teaches Us How to Pray

What do we learn from Jesus about prayer?

Jesus taught his followers that **prayer** is talking and listening to God. It is raising your mind and heart to God. When Jesus' followers asked him to teach them how to pray, he taught them the **Lord's Prayer**.

Catholic Faith Words

prayer talking and listening to God. It is raising your mind and heart to God.

Lord's Prayer the prayer that Jesus taught his disciples to pray to God the Father

Underline what we ask for in the Lord's Prayer.

 God's Word

The Lord's Prayer

This is how you are to pray:
Our Father in heaven,
hallowed be your name,
your kingdom come,
your will be done,
on earth as in heaven.
Give us today our daily bread;
and forgive us our debts,
as we forgive our debtors;
and do not subject us to the final test,
but deliver us from the evil one.

Matthew 6:9–13

How to Pray

The Lord's Prayer is also called the Our Father. It is a summary of all that we need to live a Christian life. Jesus told his disciples to call upon God the Father, as he did. He also gave the advice below.

Jesus taught his disciples how to pray to God the Father.

God's Word

Praying Well

Jesus told his disciples to pray quietly to the Father. God will hear you. Some people think that God will hear them better if they use lots of fancy words to pray. Do not be like that. The Father knows what is in your heart even before you say it. **Based on Matthew 6:6–8**

➡ **Where and for what do you pray most often?**

Share Your Faith

Think Do you have a quiet place in which to pray? Describe what you would like to have in your ideal prayer space.

_____

_____

_____

Share With a partner, share your ideas for quiet "prayer places."

Ways We Pray

What are some different ways to pray?

Circle some times when Jesus prayed.

Prayer was an important part of Jesus' life. Sometimes he got up early to pray. At other times, he prayed all night. Jesus prayed for other people. He also prayed when he needed help.

Prayer should be an important part of your day, too. You can use your own words or prayers that you have memorized. You can even pray without words by simply being quiet in the presence of God's love. But whenever you pray, you can be sure that many other Christians are praying at the very same time.

You don't ever have to worry that your prayers won't be heard. No matter where, when, or how you pray, God is always listening. Even if you are loud or very quiet, he can always hear your prayers.

We can pray anywhere and at anytime. God always hears us.

Prayer Forms

We pray for different reasons. To help you understand prayer better, here are five types, or forms, of prayer.

Catholic Faith Words

blessing and adoration in this prayer form, we show that we understand God is the Creator of all and that we need him. We give him respect and honor his greatness.

praise in this prayer form, we give God honor and thanks because he is God

petition in this prayer form, we ask God for what we need

intercession in this prayer form, we ask God to help others

thanksgiving in this prayer form, we give thanks to God for all he has given us

Connect Your Faith

Identify Prayers Work with a partner to find these Scripture verses. Tell which form of prayer each verse shows.

Psalm 51:3–5: _____

Psalm 107:1: _____

Psalm 125:4: _____

We pray with our families to give thanks and to ask for God's blessings for ourselves and others.

Our Catholic Life

How can you communicate with God?

You have conversations with God when you pray. He is always with you and hears your prayers. There are many ways to communicate with him. There are different ways to pray.

Write some more ways you can pray.

Ways to Pray

You can pray during the day by offering your good works to God.

You can use your own words to pray. God hears simple prayers, such as "Help, please," or "Thank you, Lord."

You can pray by using traditional Church prayers, such as the Lord's Prayer or prayers from Mass.

You can pray by sitting and listening to God.

You can pray with your family or with friends.

_____

_____

_____

People of Faith

Saint Gertrude the Great, 1256–c.1302

November 16

Saint Gertrude was a German nun. Her parents died when she was very young, so she lived in a convent. Gertrude was very smart and loved to read. She was especially good at reading Latin, but she liked to read all different kinds of books. Another thing Gertrude loved to do was pray. She especially liked to pray for people who had died, asking God to take them to Heaven. She prayed for her family, her friends, and everyone she met. Many other Saints have used Saint Gertrude as an example of a very holy woman.

Discuss: Who do you like to pray for?

 Learn more about Saint Gertrude at **aliveinchrist.osv.com**

Live Your Faith

Make a Prayer Wheel
Write the name of a prayer you know in each section of the wheel. Use a pencil as a spinner and recite the prayer your eraser points to.

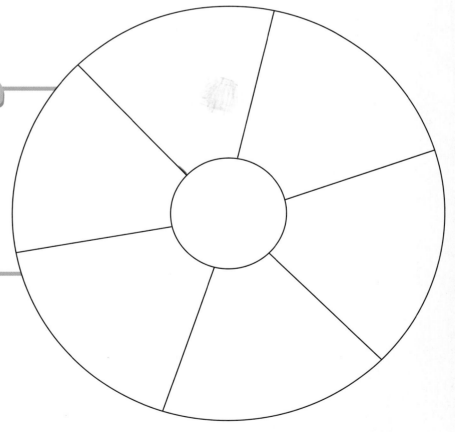

♥ Let Us Pray

Prayer of Petition

Gather and begin with the Sign of the Cross.

Group 1: Help us remember to bless and adore you.

All: Our help comes from the Lord, who made Heaven and Earth. **Based on Psalm 121**

Group 2: Help us remember to praise you,
for you are wonderful.

All: Our help comes from the Lord, who made Heaven and Earth.

Group 1: Help us remember to turn to you
whenever we need help.

All: Our help comes from the Lord, who made Heaven and Earth.

Group 2: Help us remember to thank you,
for you are so good to us.

All: Our help comes from the Lord, who made Heaven and Earth.

Leader: Let us pray.

Bow your head as the leader prays.

All: Amen.

 Sing "Open My Eyes"

FAMILY + FAITH
LIVING AND LEARNING TOGETHER

YOUR CHILD LEARNED >>>

This chapter describes prayer as talking and listening to God and the ways Jesus taught us to pray, including the Lord's Prayer. It identifies the various ways we pray.

God's Word

 Read **Matthew 6:9–13**, the Lord's Prayer. Pray with your family and talk about what the prayer means to you.

Catholics Believe

- Prayer is the raising of one's mind and heart to God.
- Prayer is an important part of a Catholic's daily life.

To learn more, go to the *Catechism of the Catholic Church* #2559, 2659 at **usccb.org**.

People of Faith

This week, your child met Saint Gertrude the Great, patron of Latin scholars. Gertrude is a model of intercessory prayer for those who have died.

CHILDREN AT THIS AGE >>>

How They Understand Prayer Third-graders are capable of talking with Jesus as a friend. This is a good time to encourage your child to speak to God in his or her own words. The social nature of third-graders also makes them especially amenable to praying with the family or in groups if they are given the structure and guidance necessary to do so. Take some time for family prayer, and encourage your child to take the lead.

CONSIDER THIS >>>

How necessary is it to be open to what someone has to say?

Real communication requires an openness of mind and heart. Opening our minds and hearts to hear what God has to say is the root of the sacred practice of prayer. "The *Catechism* reminds us that the Lord Jesus asks us to believe in order to pray and to pray in order to believe. There is a complementarity in which knowing and loving God support each other. Belief in the Father, Son, and Spirit should be essentially and immediately connected to a prayerful and loving communion with the Trinity" (*USCCA*, p. 491).

LET'S TALK >>>

- Ask your child to talk about the things that he or she prays about most often.
- Talk about the different places you pray throughout the day.

LET'S PRAY >>>

 Dear God, please bless everyone in my family, especially (mention family members here). Amen.

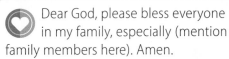 For a multimedia glossary of Catholic Faith Words, Sunday readings, seasonal and Saint resources, and chapter activities go to **aliveinchrist.osv.com**.

Chapter 6 Review

A **Work with Words** Match the description in Column A with the correct word in Column B.

Column A   Column B

1. Asking God to help other   blessing and
   people   adoration

2. Telling God that you are   praise
   grateful for his gifts

3. Honoring God's greatness   petition

4. Asking God to help you   intercession

5. Thanking God because   thanksgiving
   he's God

B **Check Understanding** Fill in the circle beside the correct answer.

6. The prayer that Jesus taught his followers is called the _____.
   ○ Lord's Prayer   ○ Hail Mary   ○ Apostles' Creed

7. Talking and listening to God is called _____.
   ○ liturgy   ○ Mass   ○ prayer

8. You can use your own words or traditional Church prayers
   that you have _____ to pray.
   ○ forgotten   ○ memorized   ○ invented

9. Which person said that God knows what is in your heart
   even before you say it?
   ○ Peter   ○ Jesus   ○ John

10. The Lord's Prayer is also called the _____.
    ○ Our Father   ○ Hail Mary   ○ Glory Be to
                                                                the Father

Go to **aliveinchrist.osv.com**
for an interactive review.

A **Work with Words** Fill in the blank with the correct word from the Word Bank.

Word Bank

blessing

praise

petition

intercession

thanksgiving

1. Which form of prayer asks God for what we

   need? _____

2. Which form of prayer asks God to help other

   people? _____

3. Which form of prayer thanks God for all the good

   things in your life? _____

4. Which form of prayer honors God because he's God? _____

5. Which form of prayer honors God's greatness? _____

B **Check Understanding** Complete each sentence by circling the correct word.

6. The Holy Trinity is the one God in _____ Divine Persons.

   three   two

7. Catholics believe in the _____ of faith without completely understanding them.

   questions   mysteries

8. The Church requires that you receive Holy Communion at least once each year during the _____ season.

   Easter   Christmas

9. Catholics must attend _____ on Sundays, or Saturday evenings, and Holy Days of Obligation.

   meetings   Mass

10. The Blessed Sacrament is reserved in the _____.

    Rectory   Tabernacle

Complete each sentence by filling in the circle next to the correct answer.

11. The _____ Creed is one of the Church's oldest creeds.

○ Jesus   ○ Gospel   ○ Apostles'

12. A _____ is a spiritual truth that is hard to understand, but is known through faith.

○ mystery   ○ prayer   ○ responsibility

13. _____ are statements of basic beliefs of the Church.

○ Sacraments   ○ Mysteries   ○ Creeds

14. You _____ by honoring and praising God.

○ worship   ○ listen   ○ have authority

15. The Holy Eucharist is also called the Blessed _____.

○ Creed   ○ Mystery   ○ Sacrament

C **Make Connections** Write responses on the lines below.

16. What are two ways that you can pray?

_____

_____

17. Why is it important for you to go to Mass?

_____

_____

18. When might you say a prayer of intercession?

_____

_____

19. How do you worship God?

_____

_____

20. When might you say a prayer of blessing?

_____

_____

Word Bank

Trinity

petition

creed

liturgy

mystery

Circle the words from the Word Bank in the word search.

21–25.

D	E	E	R	C	A	L	V
P	E	T	I	T	I	O	N
Y	T	I	N	I	R	T	G
C	M	D	L	Q	U	O	F
D	Z	E	E	E	K	R	R
A	F	I	M	O	V	X	V
N	L	I	T	U	R	G	Y
M	Y	S	T	E	R	Y	H

Jesus Christ

Our Catholic Tradition

- Jesus brought people the Good News of the Kingdom of God. (CCC, 542)

- Jesus sacrificed his own life to save everyone from sin. (CCC, 613)

- By his life, Death, Resurrection, and Ascension, Jesus Christ gives all people the gift of new life with God that will last forever. (CCC, 571)

- The Church continues to spread Christ's message of new life and hope. (CCC, 863)

What do we learn from the Gospels about Jesus' sacrifice of love?

© Our Sunday Visitor

The Good News

 Let Us Pray

Leader: Dear God, help us to follow you always.

"You will show me the path to life,
abounding joy in your presence,
the delights at your right hand forever."
Psalm 16:11

All: Jesus, give us the courage to speak about your forgiving love. Amen.

 **God's Word**

A woman had ten coins and lost one. She swept the house carefully searching until she found it. When she did, she called together her friends and neighbors and said to them, "Rejoice with me because I have found the coin that I lost." Like the woman, the angels of God will rejoice over someone who asks forgiveness for their sin. **Based on Luke 15:8–10**

? What Do You Wonder?

- Is it hard for God to forgive?
- Does God help doctors and nurses heal sick people today?

The Gospel Message

What Good News does Jesus share?

© Our Sunday Visitor

Jesus came to share Good News with us. The news that God the Father loves his People and saves them from the power of sin and everlasting death.

Just as Jesus shares the Good News of God's love with you, you pass it on to others. The work of the Catholic Church is to share the Good News of Jesus Christ in words and actions.

Another word for Good News is **Gospel**. The Church gives this name to the four books of the New Testament that tell about Jesus' life, teachings, Death, and Resurrection. The Gospels are named for Matthew, Mark, Luke, and John. They are the most important books for the Church because they focus on Jesus.

Readings from the Bible, also called Scripture, are used every time the Church community gathers to worship. Scripture readings were used to worship in Jesus' day, too.

The New Testament

Jesus' Message

When Jesus started his ministry in Nazareth, he used Hebrew Scriptures people knew to tell about his role in God's plan.

The people were surprised by Jesus' message. They were waiting for a **Messiah**, or savior. They did not expect him to be a man from Nazareth.

 God's Word

The Rejection at Nazareth

One day, Jesus came back to his hometown of Nazareth. Everyone had gathered for worship. Jesus opened the Book of Isaiah and read words that described a person God promised to send.

"The Spirit of the Lord is upon me, because he has anointed me to bring glad tidings to the poor."

Jesus then said he had come to set people free and … announce a time of blessings from God.

Then Jesus surprised everyone. He said, "Today this scripture passage is fulfilled in your hearing."

Based on Luke 4:16–21

Catholic Faith Words

Messiah the promised one who would lead his People. The word Messiah means "God's anointed," or "God's chosen one." Jesus is the Messiah.

Underline why Jesus came and what he was anointed to do.

Share Your Faith

Think List words to describe the Good News.

1. _____   3. _____

2. _____   4. _____

Share In small groups, write a radio commercial using the words you each listed.

The Kingdom of God

Where can we find God's Kingdom?

© Our Sunday Visitor

The reading from the Gospel of Luke tells of how Jesus began his work among the people. He called people to turn back to God and live as believers. He taught about God the Father's forgiveness and showed people to trust in and rely on the Father.

The words Jesus read from Scripture tell about the **Kingdom of God**, or God's reign of love, peace, and justice. In God's Kingdom, those who are poor hear joyful news. No one is a prisoner of sin and sadness. People who are sick are healed.

God's Kingdom is in Heaven and also on Earth. In the Lord's Prayer, Jesus prayed that the Father's will would be done "on earth as it is in heaven." Jesus established the Kingdom of God on Earth, and his teaching and **miracles** were signs of the Kingdom that continues to grow. When we tell others about Jesus, show God's love, and act with peace, we work with God to help his Reign spread.

Catholic Faith Words

Kingdom of God the world of love, peace, and justice that is in Heaven and is still being built on Earth

miracle something that cannot be explained by science, but happened by the power of God

Circle what Jesus called people to do.

124

Parables

Jesus often taught with **parables**. Parables are short teaching stories that Jesus used to teach us about God. One day, Jesus told this story.

God's Word

The Mustard Seed

Jesus said that the Kingdom of God was like a mustard seed. This seed grows from a tiny seed into a large, beautiful tree.   Based on Mark 4:30–32

Jesus was planting the seed of the Kingdom. Jesus showed people how to live. He healed people and set them free from loneliness, sorrow, and sin. He helped people see and feel God's love. Jesus sends his Church to invite everyone into God's Kingdom.

Some other parables Jesus told were the Parable of the Lost Sheep, the Parable of the Good Samaritan, and the Parable of the Great Feast. He told these stories to teach people about God's love and how to treat one another with kindness and respect. Jesus taught that everyone is welcome in God's Kingdom.

© Our Sunday Visitor

Catholic Faith Words

parable a short story Jesus told about everyday life to teach something about God

Connect Your Faith

Share Examples Who are some people who have taught you about God's love? Name one thing you learned from each of them.

Our Catholic Life

What do the parables really mean?

Jesus told many parables to help people learn about God. Sometimes you must think and study to understand what these stories mean.

One way to understand parables is to look for the symbols in them. The next time you read a parable, look for the symbols and think about what they stand for. Different people may get different meanings from the same story.

Draw symbols from Jesus' parables.

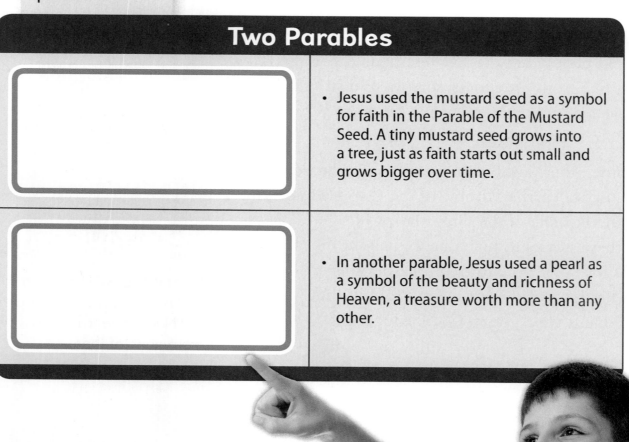

Two Parables

- Jesus used the mustard seed as a symbol for faith in the Parable of the Mustard Seed. A tiny mustard seed grows into a tree, just as faith starts out small and grows bigger over time.

- In another parable, Jesus used a pearl as a symbol of the beauty and richness of Heaven, a treasure worth more than any other.

People of Faith

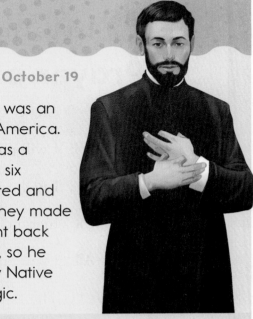

Saint Isaac Jogues, 1607–1646

October 19

Saint Isaac Jogues was a Jesuit priest in France. He was an explorer and wanted to bring the Gospel to North America. He sailed across the ocean to Canada. There, he was a missionary to the Native Americans where he spent six years preaching the Gospel. Saint Isaac was captured and tortured by some people who were afraid of him. They made him a slave. He was freed by Dutch settlers and went back to France. He still wanted to spread the Good News, so he returned to Canada. Sadly, Saint Isaac was killed by Native Americans who thought he was practicing bad magic.

Discuss: Talk about a time when you told someone about Jesus.

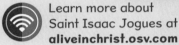

Learn more about Saint Isaac Jogues at **aliveinchrist.osv.com**

Live Your Faith

List three ways you can work with God as he builds his Kingdom.

1. _____

2. _____

3. _____

Write one thing you can do this week to invite others to be part of God's Kingdom?

_____

_____

_____

_____

Let Us Pray

Prayer of Praise

Gather and begin with the Sign of the Cross.

All: I will praise your name, my King and my God.

Side 1: I will give you glory, my God and King.

Side 2: Every day I will bless and praise your name forever.

All: I will praise your name, my King and my God.

Side 1: The Lord is full of grace and mercy.

Side 2: He is good in all his works and full of compassion.

All: I will praise your name, my King and my God.

Side 1: The Lord is faithful and always near. His name is holy.

Side 2: He lifts up those who fall.

All: I will praise your name, my King and my God.
Based on Psalm 145

Leader: Let us pray.

All: Amen.

Bow your head as the leader prays.

Sing "When We Praise You"
We praise you,
we bless you,
we adore you,
and give glory to you
our God.
© 2011, John Burland. All rights reserved.

FAMILY+FAITH
LIVING AND LEARNING TOGETHER

YOUR CHILD LEARNED >>>

This chapter explains the Good News that God the Father loves his People and saves them from the power of sin and everlasting death. It also explains that the Gospels in the New Testament tell the stories of Jesus' life and teachings, parables, and miracles.

God's Word

 Read **Luke 15:8–10** and talk about what these verses mean to you.

Catholics Believe

• Jesus taught about God's Kingdom of love, peace, and justice that is in Heaven and is still being built on Earth.

• Jesus established the Kingdom of God on Earth, and his teaching and miracles were signs of the Kingdom.

To learn more, go to the *Catechism of the Catholic Church* #546, 1154 at usccb.org.

People of Faith

This week, your child met Saint Isaac Jogues, one of the first martyrs in North America.

CHILDREN AT THIS AGE >>>

How They Understand The Gospel Third-graders don't often pause to wonder where the accounts of Jesus' life came from or why we have four Gospels in Scripture, told from different perspectives. As they get to know the Gospels better, they will become more aware of the different tones and character of the Gospel writers and the differences that arise from the stories having been told for different audiences.

CONSIDER THIS >>>

When you pray "thy kingdom come," how do you think that's going to happen?

Reflecting on the Kingdom of God requires us to keep one foot in the present and another in the future. We manifest, or participate as members of the Kingdom, when we live as disciples of Christ. The Kingdom is "the Good News that results in love, justice, and mercy for the whole world. The Kingdom is realized partially on earth and permanently in heaven. We enter this Kingdom through faith in Christ, baptismal initiation into the Church, and life in communion with all her members" (*USCCA, 79–80*).

LET'S TALK >>>

• Ask your child to name some ways he or she can share the Good News.

• Talk about some of your favorite parables and what they mean to you.

LET'S PRAY >>>

 Saint Isaac, pray for us that we may have the courage to bring God's love to others. Amen.

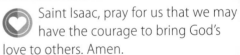 For a multimedia glossary of Catholic Faith Words, Sunday readings, seasonal and Saint resources, and chapter activities go to **aliveinchrist.osv.com**.

Chapter 7 Review

A **Work with Words** Complete each sentence with the correct answer.

1. God's _____ is in Heaven and also on Earth.

2. The _____ is God's promised one.

3. Jesus used _____ to teach others about God.

4. The word Gospel means _____.

5. Jesus' _____ happened by the power of God.

B **Check Understanding** To complete each statement use the same answer at the end of the first sentence and beginning of the second sentence.

6. Parables are stories told by _____.

   _____ set people free from injustice and sin.

7. Jesus taught about the _____. The

   _____ is God's world of love, peace, and

   justice that is in Heaven and is still being built on Earth.

8. The books in the New Testament that tell stories of Jesus

   are the _____. The _____

   are named for Matthew, Mark, Luke, and John.

9. Readings from the Bible are also called

   _____. _____ was an

   important part of worship in Jesus' day.

10. Jesus is the _____. _____

    is a Hebrew word that means "God's anointed."

Go to **aliveinchrist.osv.com** for an interactive review.

The Paschal Mystery

♥ Let Us Pray

Leader: Loving God, help us to give of ourselves.

"Offer praise as your sacrifice to God;
fulfill your vows to the Most High."
Psalm 50:14

All: As we think about your great sacrifice on the Cross, Jesus, we cannot imagine how great your love is for us. Fill us with your love today. Amen.

📖 God's Word

Jesus was talking to the disciples at the Last Supper. He said, "This is my commandment: love one another as I love you. No one has greater love than this, to lay down one's life for one's friends." Based on John 15:12–13

❓ What Do You Wonder?

- Each time you go to Communion, is Jesus really offering his love to you?

- How can you love others as Jesus loves you?

Being True to Our Promises

What does it mean to make a sacrifice?

Jesus made a promise to his Father. A promise can be easy or difficult to keep. You may need to give something up to keep a promise. Read this story about keeping promises.

Lindsey's Promise

One day, Lindsey was faced with a difficult choice. She was having fun with her friend when suddenly she stopped and looked at her watch.

"It's late. I have to go," Lindsey said.

"Call and say you're playing," Sarah said.

"I made a promise. I have to go," Lindsey said.

At the care center, Aunt Diane smiled brightly. "Hello, Lindsey. I am so glad to see you!"

"I promised to go for a walk with you."

Aunt Diane smiled and said, "Great! Let's go!"

© Our Sunday Visitor

Catholic Faith Words

sacrifice giving up something out of love for someone else or for the common good (the good of everyone). Jesus sacrificed his life for all people.

Circle what Lindsey promised.

Sacrifices Show Love

Lindsey gave up an afternoon with a friend because she made a promise. When you give up something or do something difficult out of love, it is called a **sacrifice**. It is not easy to make a sacrifice. It takes a lot of love and courage. You have to be unselfish when you make a sacrifice.

Jesus chose to make the greatest sacrifice of all. He did something that no one else could do. Jesus gave up his life so that people could be saved from the power of sin and everlasting death. He freely gave up his life so that all people could have new life with God forever.

The disciples mourn and pray at the foot of the Cross.

Share Your Faith

Think When have you made a sacrifice for someone? How do sacrifices show love? How did this sacrifice make you feel?

_____

_____

_____

_____

Share your answer with a partner.

Jesus' Resurrection

What does the Paschal Mystery mean?

Jesus' loving choice fulfilled God's plan to save his People. Through the work of the Holy Spirit, the Father raised Jesus from Death to new life. This is called the **Resurrection**. The Resurrection showed that God's power is stronger than death.

Catholic Faith Words

Resurrection the event of Jesus being raised from Death to new life by God the Father through the power of the Holy Spirit

Underline what Mary Magdalene saw when she went to Jesus' tomb.

God's Word

The Appearance to Mary Magdalene

Mary Magdalene went to Jesus' tomb, but she found it empty. She thought that people had taken Jesus' body away. Then angels spoke to her, and she heard someone call her name. It was Jesus!

When Mary first saw Jesus, she didn't recognize him. Thinking that he was the gardener, she asked where Jesus was. He said, "Mary!"

Then she knew it was Jesus. He told her to tell his friends that he was returning to the Father. Mary went to the disciples and said, "I have seen the Lord," and repeated what he told her.

Based on John 20:11–18

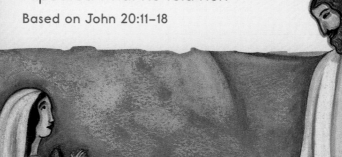

Christ's Saving Work

Jesus' suffering, Death, Resurrection, and Ascension are called the **Paschal Mystery**. The word Paschal comes from a word that means "passover." Jesus died to save people from their sins at the time of year when members of the Jewish faith celebrate Passover. Jesus was raised from the dead and at the **Ascension** returned to Heaven to be with God the Father forever. He "passed over" from death to life so that all people can have new life with God in Heaven.

The Mass and the other Sacraments are ways that the Church lives out this great mystery. When you take part in the celebration of the Eucharist, you share in the saving power of Christ's Paschal Mystery.

➡ **How is the news of Jesus' Resurrection and Ascension shared today?**

Catholic Faith Words

Ascension when the Risen Jesus was taken up to Heaven to be with God the Father forever

Paschal Mystery the mystery of Jesus' suffering, Death, Resurrection, and Ascension

Connect Your Faith

Draw a Crucifix Draw a picture of a crucifix and decorate it using words and images. Look at it during difficult times, and remember Jesus' saving actions.

Our Catholic Life

How can your sacrifices help others?

When you make a sacrifice, you are offering a special gift. Most gifts involve time, talent, or treasure. In addition to helping others, gifts of sacrifice can help you feel good about yourself.

> Write down some other ways you can share your time, talent, and treasure.

Gifts of Sacrifice

Gifts of time include paying attention to others.

- You give time when you play with a younger sister, brother, or neighbor.
- You can also visit elderly people in retirement centers.
- _____

A gift of treasure involves giving money to a worthy cause.

- You can give money to the Church or to other organizations that help people.
- You could donate some of your birthday money to the poor.
- _____

Gifts of talent include using your special abilities.

- You can give up some Saturday morning TV shows for choir practice.
- You could make cards for the elderly at a local senior center.
- _____

➔ **Why do you think gifts of sacrifice can help you become a better person?**

People of Faith

© Our Sunday Visitor

Saint Mary Magdalene, first century A.D.

July 22

Saint Mary Magdalene was sick. We don't know what was wrong, but Jesus made her well. She then became one of his followers. Mary was with Jesus as he preached about God's love. She stood at the foot of his Cross as he suffered and died. She went to Jesus' tomb on the first Easter morning and was surprised that the tomb was empty. Jesus appeared to her and told her to tell others that he had risen from the dead. Mary did as she was told. Many people believed in Jesus' Resurrection because of her.

Discuss: Who was the first one to tell you about Jesus' Resurrection?

 Learn more about Saint Mary Magdalene at **aliveinchrist.osv.com**

Live Your Faith

Find Your Treasure On the coins labeled time, talent, and treasure, write a sacrifice that you plan to make for someone.

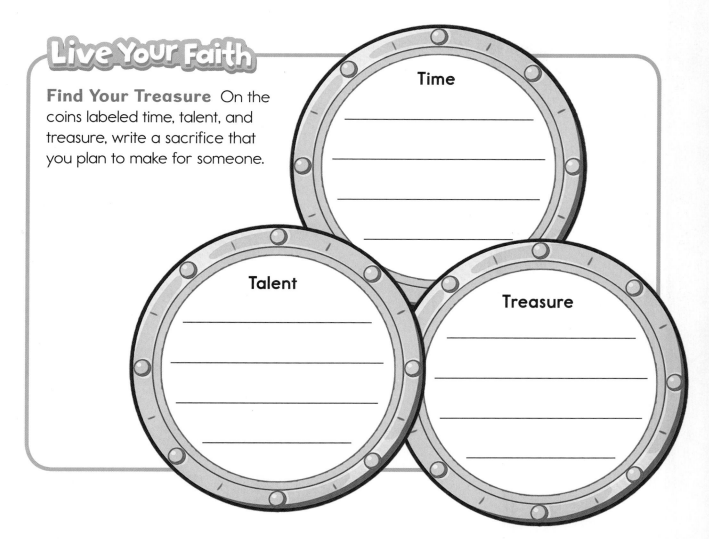

Time

_____

_____

_____

_____

Talent

_____

_____

_____

_____

Treasure

_____

_____

_____

_____

The Paschal Mystery   **137**

Let Us Pray

Act of Faith

Gather and begin with the Sign of the Cross.

All: O my God,
I firmly believe that you are one God in three divine
  Persons,
Father, Son, and Holy Spirit;
I believe that your divine Son became man,
and died for our sins,
and that he will come to judge the living and the dead.
I believe these and all the truths which the Holy Catholic
  Church teaches,
because you have revealed them,
who can neither deceive nor be deceived. Amen.

 Sing "We Proclaim Your Death, O Lord"
We proclaim your death, O Lord.
Jesus died for us.
We profess your Resurrection.
Jesus lives with us.
Until you come again,
we wait in joyful hope!
© 2011, John Burland. All rights reserved.

FAMILY+FAITH
LIVING AND LEARNING TOGETHER

YOUR CHILD LEARNED >>>

The chapter explains that Jesus sacrificed his life to save us and examines how the Church celebrates the Paschal Mystery in each of the Seven Sacraments.

God's Word

 Read **John 15:12–13** to learn more about loving one another as Jesus loves us.

Catholics Believe

• Jesus died and rose to new life to save all people from the power of sin.

• The Church celebrates the Paschal Mystery in all of the Seven Sacraments.

To learn more, go to the *Catechism of the Catholic Church* #613, 1085 at **usccb.org**.

People of Faith

This week, your child met Saint Mary Magdalene, who was one of the first people to tell others about Jesus' Resurrection.

CHILDREN AT THIS AGE >>>

How They Understand Jesus' Sacrifice It's difficult for third-graders to understand why it was necessary for Jesus to die. The suffering, Death, Resurrection, and Ascension of Jesus Christ was in atonement for the sins of all mankind. The concept of atonement is still foreign to children this age, and can be difficult for many adults as well. For now, it is helpful for your child to understand that Jesus loved us so much that he was willing to die to show his love.

CONSIDER THIS >>>

What does it mean that we daily die and rise with Christ?

Life requires many "dyings." We die to being an adolescent, we die to being responsible only for ourselves, and we die to relationships that fail. Jesus' Death and Resurrection help us to understand that in every death, God can bring new life. "Faith in the resurrection of our bodies is inseparable from our faith in the Resurrection of Christ's body from the dead. He rose as our head, as the pattern of our rising, and as the life-giving source of our new life" (*USCCA, 155*).

LET'S TALK >>>

• Ask your child how making a sacrifice for someone else can help he or she feel good about themselves.

• Talk about a time you have made a sacrifice for someone else. How did that sacrifice show love?

LET'S PRAY >>>

 Saint Mary, help us remember to ask Jesus for help when we are sick. Amen.

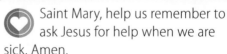 For a multimedia glossary of Catholic Faith Words, Sunday readings, seasonal and Saint resources, and chapter activities go to **aliveinchrist.osv.com**.

Chapter 8 Review

A **Work with Words** Complete the following paragraph with the correct words from the Word Bank.

1–5. Jesus made a _____ to his Father. He gave up his life so that people could be _____ from sin and everlasting _____. Jesus' _____ showed people that God's power is _____ than death.

Word Bank
....
Resurrection

death

stronger

saved

promise

B **Check Understanding** Fill in the blank with the correct answer.

6. What is it called when you give up something out of love or for a greater good? _____

7. What is the word that means the Father raised the Risen Jesus to new life by the work of the Holy Spirit? _____

8. Who told the disciples the news that Jesus was returning to the Father? _____

9. The mystery of Jesus' suffering, Death, Resurrection, and Ascension is called the _____.

10. You share in the Paschal Mystery when you participate in the _____.

© Our Sunday Visitor

Go to **aliveinchrist.osv.com** for an interactive review.

The Body of Christ

 ## Let Us Pray

Leader: Loving God, bring hope and comfort to all people.

"Defend the lowly and fatherless;
render justice to the afflicted and needy."
Psalm 82:3

All: You are the source of all hope. So many people in the world need basic things, or they are lonely or sad. Give me the eyes to see and the heart to act as your Son did. Amen.

God's Word

The Holy Spirit gives us different kinds of gifts and different ways of serving. But, there is only one Lord. There are different ways to use your gifts, but it is God who gives them to each of us. Based on 1 Corinthians 12:4–7

 ? What Do You Wonder?

- How did God decide what gifts to give you?

- What happens when you only use your gifts to make things better for yourself?

We Each Have a Role

How do we continue Jesus' work today?

When people work together, the job is easier for everyone. God's Word tells us that we all have different gifts and talents we use together for the good of the Church.

The Church

The people of the Church work together. When Jesus lived on Earth, he did his Father's work. The Holy Spirit was with Jesus. At his Ascension, Jesus returned to his Father in Heaven. Then Jesus sent the Spirit to be with his Church. The Holy Spirit makes it possible for the Church to continue Jesus' work today.

As a baptized member of the Church family, you are part of a **parish**. Together as a community and as an individual, you are Jesus to other people. You use your hands and feet, your mouth and ears, and your mind and heart to do Jesus' work.

One name for the Church is the **Body of Christ**. This name tells you that all Church members are one body. Even though each member of the Church is unique, we are all one, just like the parts of a body are different parts of one body. We each have a special part to play in God's plan. This name also says that you belong to Jesus. Jesus is the head, and we follow him.

Catholic Faith Words

parish the local community of Catholics that meets at a particular place

Body of Christ a name for the Church of which Christ is the head. All the baptized are members of the Body.

Draw a box around another name for the Church.

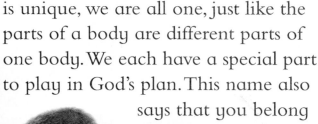

Doing Jesus' Work

The Church continues to do Jesus' work on Earth. Jesus' mission was to help people know and give glory to God the Father. An important part of his work was caring for people who needed help.

As a Church, we continue Jesus' work by helping people know and worship God and also by caring for people who need help.

Saint Francis of Assisi taught that people can come to know God through our love for them. He said, "Preach the Gospel at all times. When necessary, use words." We can help fulfill Jesus' mission with our actions and our deeds.

Members of parishes work together to help others in need and show love for God and others.

We help others know God when we are good examples, make right choices, and put God first. When we work together to help others in need, we show love for them and for God. Someday someone might ask you to explain why you live the way you do. When you talk about your love for God, you help others know him.

Share Your Faith

Think What would you say if someone asked why you love God? Write a poem using the words you used to describe your love for God.

_____

_____

_____

Share With a partner, share your reasons for living the way you do.

Sharing in Jesus' Work of Helping Others

How can we respond to Jesus' call to help others?

Jesus wants us to show love and care for everyone. In the story below, Jesus speaks of himself as a king, who praises those who have treated strangers and neighbors like they were Jesus himself. Jesus told his followers this story to teach them how they should treat others.

Underline what Jesus will say to some people at the end of time.

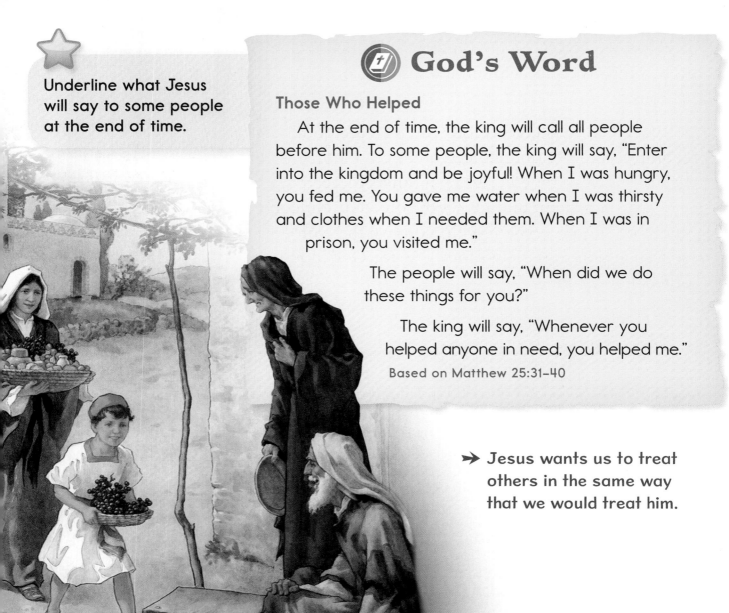

🔲 God's Word

Those Who Helped

At the end of time, the king will call all people before him. To some people, the king will say, "Enter into the kingdom and be joyful! When I was hungry, you fed me. You gave me water when I was thirsty and clothes when I needed them. When I was in prison, you visited me."

The people will say, "When did we do these things for you?"

The king will say, "Whenever you helped anyone in need, you helped me."

Based on Matthew 25:31–40

➤ Jesus wants us to treat others in the same way that we would treat him.

Share Your Gifts

God gave each person special gifts, or talents. A talent is something you enjoy doing and can do well. You are called to use your talents to serve others. When you do this, you are being a good steward of the gifts that God has given you. **Stewardship** helps us have thankful hearts and a commitment to sharing our gifts with others.

When people put their talents together and work as the Body of Christ, they can do more than any one person can do alone.

At the end of Mass, you go forth to do Jesus' work in the world. The priest or deacon says, "Go in peace, glorifying the Lord by your life." You glorify the Lord by making good choices, by helping people know God, and by loving and serving all of God's people.

➜ **How many different talents can you count among the people around you?**

Catholic Faith Words

stewardship the way we appreciate and use God's gifts, including our time, talent, and treasure and the resources of creation

Connect Your Faith

Ways to Help Draw one way you help people worship God at your parish.

Our Catholic Life

How does your parish share in Jesus' work?

As a way to continue Jesus' work, parishes teach people about God the Father's great love and help those in need. This work can be done in the parish, in the community, or even in another country.

Get Involved

Your parish is already working to bring hope and understanding to your community and the world. Some ways that parishes get involved are listed below.

Place a check mark next to the ways you can or will get involved.

Get Involved

☐ Collect money for the missions.

☐ Serve food in a homeless shelter.

☐ Become an altar server.

☐ Start a collection of baby items for a women's shelter.

☐ Invite a friend to come to Mass or help someone get religious education class.

☐ Clean a park.

☐ Offer to help at computer classes for senior citizens.

☐ Sing in the choir or play an instrument at Mass.

☐ Become a greeter with your family.

☐ Check your parish bulletin or website for announcements about your parish's involvement in the community.

People of Faith

Blessed Joseph Vaz, 1651–1711   January 16

Blessed Joseph Vaz was born in India. Most people in India are Hindu. Joseph's family was Catholic. He wanted to share the Gospel with everyone. He used his gifts to help other people know God. He went to faraway places to teach about Jesus and build churches. Joseph decided to become a missionary and went to Ceylon (now Sri Lanka), even though the government there didn't allow priests in the country. Joseph helped bring others there to talk about Jesus and serve God's People.

Discuss: What are some things you can do to help others know God?

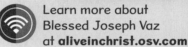
Learn more about Blessed Joseph Vaz at **aliveinchrist.osv.com**

Live Your Faith

Share Your Talents Make a banner to encourage people to use their talents to help one another as members of the Body of Christ.

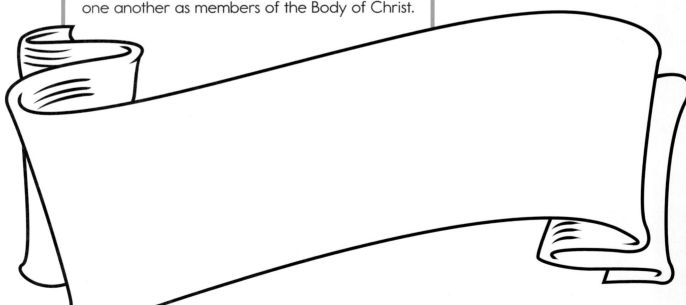

Let Us Pray

Prayer of Petition

Gather and begin with the Sign of the Cross.

Leader: God our Father, we stand before you
as the Body of Christ.

Reader 1: Help our eyes see work that needs to be done,

All: So that we can share in your work.

Reader 2: Help our ears hear your wisdom written in Scripture,

All: So that we can praise God and listen to his will.

Reader 1: Help our hands and feet be strong,

All: So that we can help one another.

Reader 2: Help our hearts be full of love,

All: So that we can share your love.

Leader: Let us pray.

Bow your heads as the leader prays.

All: Amen.

 Sing "Somos el Cuerpo de Cristo/We Are the Body of Christ"
Somos el Cuerpo de Cristo.
We are the Body of Christ.
Hemos oído el llamado;
we've answered "Yes" to the call of the Lord.
Somos el Cuerpo de Cristo.
We are the Body of Christ.
Traemos su santo mensaje.
We come to bring the Good News to the world.
© 1994, Jaime Cortez. Published by OCP. All rights reserved.

FAMILY+FAITH
LIVING AND LEARNING TOGETHER

YOUR CHILD LEARNED >>>

This chapter explains that all baptized Catholics are members of the Body of Christ and examines how people use their gifts and talents to serve God and others.

God's Word

 Read **1 Corinthians 12:4–7** and talk about how your family is part of the Body of Christ.

Catholics Believe

- The Church is the Body of Christ, to which all her members belong.
- Stewardship is the way we appreciate and use God's gifts—including our time, talent, and treasure and the gift of creation—to serve God and others.

To learn more, go to the *Catechism of the Catholic Church* #521, 1267 at **usccb.org**.

People of Faith

This week, your child met Blessed Joseph Vaz, a priest from India who traveled to other countries to help others know about God.

CHILDREN AT THIS AGE >>>

How They Understand Participation in Jesus' Work Third-graders are sometimes initially surprised when they realize they can participate in God's work and that, in fact, everyone in the Church, young and old, has particular work to do. This is a good time in your child's life to present this concept, as he or she is now also becoming more aware of ways to be helpful at home and at school.

CONSIDER THIS >>>

How do you foster your child's gifts and talents? Do you connect them to God's gifts and will for him/her?

As Catholic parents, we balance competition and the common good. It requires helping our children to become their personal best and helping them understand that this talent or gift has been given for the good of the community. "…it is fitting that parents always encourage their children to make life decisions with serious consideration about the best ways to live out their faith" (*USCCA, p. 379*).

LET'S TALK >>>

- Ask your child how he or she can help Jesus by helping someone else.
- Talk about a time when you've shared your talents to help others. What did you do and how did it help someone else?

LET'S PRAY >>>

 Blessed Joseph Vaz, pray for us that we may help others know God. Amen.

 For a multimedia glossary of Catholic Faith Words, Sunday readings, seasonal and Saint resources, and chapter activities go to **aliveinchrist.osv.com**.

Chapter 9 Review

A **Work with Words** Complete each sentence with the correct word or words from the Word Bank.

Word Bank

Church

stewardship

Body of Christ

Holy Spirit

glorify

1. The Church is sometimes called the

   _____.

2. You can _____ the Lord by making good choices and helping people to know God.

3. Since Jesus returned to his Father, the

   _____ continues his work on Earth.

4. When Jesus returned to Heaven, he sent the

   _____ to be with his followers.

5. _____ means appreciating and using God's gift of creation, including our time, talent, and treasure.

B **Check Understanding** Complete each sentence.

Column A	Column B
6. The Church continues Jesus' work with the help of	many members.
7. The Church is one, but it has	the Holy Spirit.
8. At his Ascension, Jesus returned to his	Baptism.
9. Your parish is a community that continues	Father in Heaven.
10. We become members of the Body of Christ at	Jesus' work.

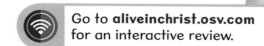
Go to **aliveinchrist.osv.com** for an interactive review.

© Our Sunday Visitor

A **Work with Words** Match each description in Column A with the correct term in Column B.

Column A   Column B

1. Jesus' teaching stories   Messiah

2. Jesus made a great   Paschal Mystery

3. A name for the Church, of   parables
which Christ is the head

4. A Hebrew word that means   Body of Christ
"anointed"

5. Jesus' suffering, Death,   sacrifice
Resurrection, and Ascension

Fill in the circle beside the correct answer.

6. The four books about Jesus in the New Testament are the _____.

  ○ parables   ○ Gospels   ○ Bibles

7. The Kingdom of God is also called God's _____.

  ○ law   ○ promise   ○ reign of love

8. What happened three days after Jesus' Death?

  ○ Resurrection   ○ Visitation   ○ Ascension

9. The Gospels are named for Matthew, Mark, Luke, and _____.

  ○ James   ○ Joseph   ○ John

10. Whom did Jesus send to us after he returned to Heaven?

  ○ Holy Spirit   ○ Apostles   ○ Mary

B **Check Understanding** Complete each sentence
with the correct word from the Word Bank.

Word Bank

Heaven

talents

Passover

Baptism

me

11. The word Paschal comes from a word that
means

_____.

12. Jesus passed over from Death to life so that all
people can have life with God in

_____.

13. Catholics become members of the Body of Christ at

_____.

14. Jesus said, "Whenever you helped anyone in need, you helped

_____."

15. The Church has many members with special gifts, or

_____.

Write the letter T if the sentence is TRUE. Write the letter F is the sentence
is FALSE.

16. ☐ The Gospel message is the Good News of God's Kingdom.

17. ☐ A miracle is something that can be explained by science.

18. ☐ Jesus used a pearl as a symbol of the beauty of Heaven.

19. ☐ After the Resurrection, Jesus told Mary Magdalene to tell
others that he was returning to God the Father.

20. ☐ Stewardship means keeping God's gifts to ourselves.

C **Make Connections** Write responses on the lines below.

21. In your own words, explain the Kingdom of God.

_____

_____

_____

22. What does the word Ascension mean?

_____

_____

23. What does it mean to you to be a part of the Body of Christ?

_____

_____

24. Why did Jesus say, "Whenever you helped anyone in need, you helped me"?

_____

_____

25. How can you use your talents to help others?

_____

_____

The Church

Our Catholic Tradition

- The Holy Spirit is the soul of the Mystical Body of Christ, the Church, and unites us. (CCC, 809)

- The Church is one and holy because she is united in the Trinity and to Christ. (CCC, 813–822)

- The Church is catholic, or universal, because she has all the truths and means of salvation. (CCC, 823–829)

- The Church is apostolic—founded by Jesus on Peter and the Apostles. The Pope and bishops lead the Church. (CCC, 857–865)

How does the power of the Holy Spirit work in the Church through her bishops and all Catholics?

Saint Peter's Basilica Vatican City in Rome, Italy

© Our Sunday Visitor

Church Leaders

♥ Let Us Pray

Leader: Caring God, help us follow your will for our lives.

"With your counsel you guide me,
and at the end receive me with honor."
Psalm 73:24

All: Jesus, you give us leaders to help us stay close to you. We give thanks for the priests and deacons who serve you by serving our Church. Amen.

📖 God's Word

Jesus sent out the Twelve and told them to tell others, "The kingdom of heaven is at hand." He told them that they didn't need to take any money, or a sack to carry their things. He told them not to take extra clothes or shoes. They would depend on others for what they needed. **Based on Matthew 10:5–10**

❓ What Do You Wonder?

- How do you think the Apostles felt when Jesus said they had to depend on others?

- Why do pastors need the help of others?

The First Leader

What special job did Jesus choose Peter for?

Here is a story about Saint Peter, the first leader of the Catholic Church.

© Our Sunday Visitor

Catholic Faith Words

Pope the successor of Peter, the bishop of Rome, and the head of the entire Catholic Church

God's Word

Peter's Belief

Jesus asked his disciples, "But who do you say that I am?" Simon answered him, "You are the Messiah, the Son of the living God." Then Jesus blessed Simon and told him that he could not know that from being human. Only his Father could make that known. "And so I say to you, you are Peter, and upon this rock I will build my church."

Peter Denies Jesus

A servant asked him if he had been with Jesus, but Peter denied that he had been with him. Two other people asked Peter if he was friends with Jesus, and Peter denied Jesus again both times.

Then a rooster crowed, and Peter remembered what Jesus had told him: "Before the cock crows you will deny me three times." Peter went out and began to weep bitterly.

Jesus and Peter

After his Resurrection, Jesus showed himself to his followers. Jesus asked Peter if he loved him. Peter responded yes, I love you. Jesus said to him, "Feed my lambs." Jesus asked Peter again, "Do you love me?" Peter answered, "Yes, Lord, you know that I love you." Jesus said, "Tend my sheep" and asked a third time, "Do you love me?" Peter said, "Lord, you know everything; you know that I love you." [Jesus] said to him, "Feed my sheep." Based on Matthew 16:15–19, 26:69–75, John 21:15–17

Jesus chose Peter to be the first leader of the Apostles and the head of the Church. The person in this position is now called the **Pope**. They are the successor of Peter. The Holy Spirit guides the Pope to help him lead the Church and care for all of God's People.

Share Your Faith

Think Have you ever been asked to be a leader?

Share Talk about your experience in leading a group. Was leading easy or difficult?

The Pope and bishops carry on the work of the Apostles, preaching the Good News. They lead, guide, and care for God's People.

Chosen to Lead

How do the Pope and bishops lead the Church?

The Apostles were the twelve men chosen by Jesus to be the first leaders of the Church, and Peter was their leader. The Apostles' teaching and authority have been handed down to the bishops, who are the leaders of the Church today. They are the people who now take the place of the Apostles on Earth. This is called **Apostolic Succession**.

The Pope is also the Bishop of Rome. The word **bishop** means "overseer." A bishop is an ordained man who helps to lead, teach, and serve a diocese. Bishops are the successors of the Apostles. We use the word **Magisterium** to talk about the teaching office of the Church, which is all of the bishops in union with the Pope.

Catholic Faith Words

Apostolic Succession the term used to describe how the authority and power to lead and teach the Church is passed down from the Apostles to their successors, the bishops

bishop an ordained man who works together with other bishops and the Pope in teaching, leading, and making the Church holy. The bishops are the successors of the Apostles.

Leaders of the Parish

Dioceses are made up of many parishes. Each parish has leaders, too. The pastor is a priest who has been given the authority to lead a parish community. He, along with other priests, celebrates the Sacraments and works with others to serve the people of a parish. Deacons celebrate some of the Sacraments and do works of charity.

Church Members Serve

There are other people in a parish who are called to serve and lead. These men and women are not ordained, but they help with many parish ministries. Your catechist (religious education teacher) is one of these people. Other examples include liturgical ministers, parish committee members, and directors of religious education and youth ministry.

➤ **What are some ways that the leaders of your parish help you?**

Catholic Faith Words

Magisterium the teaching office of the Church, which is all of the bishops in union with the Pope

Underline what a parish pastor does.

Connect Your Faith

Serving Others On the lines below, write one way that each of the Church members can serve others.

1. Pastor: _____

_____

2. Catechist: _____

_____

3. You: _____

_____

Write down one interesting thing that the Pope does for the Church.

Our Catholic Life

What is the Pope's job?

The Pope has a special job in the Church. He is guided by the Holy Spirit to lead the Church. The more you learn about the Pope, the better you will understand the Church and your role in her mission.

The Pope

The Pope teaches.
The Pope is the highest teacher and guide in the Church. The Church learns about important matters of faith from what the Pope says and what he writes.

The Pope leads.
Together with the bishops, the Pope makes decisions about what Catholics should do to be better followers of Jesus.

The Pope travels.
The Pope goes all over the world to meet Catholics and people of other faiths. He helps bring peace and understanding.

The Pope cares for the whole world.
He celebrates Mass and meets with Catholics as well as with world leaders.

_____

_____

People of Faith

Saint Gregory the Great, c. 540–604

September 3

Saint Gregory didn't want to be the Pope, but was elected Pope anyway. The Pope has a special job. He is guided by the Holy Spirit to lead the Church. Gregory was sad to give up his life as a monk, but he knew he had to do what God wanted. After he was Pope, he trained missionaries to preach the Gospel. Gregory thought beautiful music helped us pray better. Gregorian chant, a special kind of music, is named for him.

Discuss: How do you feel when you are asked to do something you don't want to do?

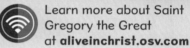

Learn more about Saint Gregory the Great at **aliveinchrist.osv.com**

Live Your Faith

My Church Community Fill in the blanks to show how you belong to the community of the Catholic Church.

My name is _____.

I belong to a parish in the (Arch)diocese of _____.

Our pastor is _____. Our (arch)bishop is

_____. Pope _____

and the bishops lead the Catholic Church.

Research Do some research with a family member to find out one thing that is unique about your parish or diocese.

Let Us Pray

Prayer of the Faithful

Gather and begin with the Sign of the Cross.

Leader: We gather today to pray for our leaders and for the needs of the Church.

Reader 1: For the Pope, the bishops, the priests, and other Church leaders, that they may act with wisdom and encourage hope, we pray to the Lord.

All: Lord, hear our prayer.

Reader 2: For our teachers and catechists, that they may help us understand your plan for us, we pray to the Lord.

All: Lord, hear our prayer.

Reader 3: For all members of the Church, that we may use our gifts to serve, we pray to the Lord.

All: Lord, hear our prayer.

Leader: Let us pray.

Bow your heads as the leader prays.

All: Amen.

 Sing "Jesus Is with Us"
Jesus is with us today,
beside us to guide us today.
Jesus teaches us, Jesus heals us,
for we are his Church; we are his chosen;
we are the children of God.
Based on Psalm 122. Text and music
© 1988, Christopher Walker.
Published by OCP.
All rights reserved.

FAMILY+FAITH
LIVING AND LEARNING TOGETHER

YOUR CHILD LEARNED >>>

This chapter explains how the Pope, bishops, and pastors lead and guide the Church and describes the Pope and bishops as successors of the Apostles.

God's Word

 Read **Matthew 10:5–10** and learn how Jesus sent the Apostles to announce the Good News.

Catholics Believe

- The bishops are the successors of the Apostles who teach, lead, and make the Church holy.
- The Pope is the successor of Peter, the bishop of Rome, and the head of the entire Church.

To learn more, go to the *Catechism of the Catholic Church* #816–939 at **usccb.org**.

People of Faith

This week, your child met Saint Gregory the Great, one of our past Popes. The Gregorian chant is named after him.

CHILDREN AT THIS AGE >>>

How They Understand Leaders in the Church The adults in the parish that interact most with children, such as the catechists and sometimes the parish priests, are usually the Church leaders of whom children are most aware. They do not yet have much exposure to the Pope or even the local bishop. However, learning more about the larger Church and her leaders can help your child feel more connected to the worldwide community of faith.

CONSIDER THIS >>>

How difficult is it to keep your whole family on the same page?

There are so many competing values and obligations in our lives. It may tend to pull the family in many directions. That is why it is important that each member of the family knows that faith is the priority in your family life. "When a family becomes a school of virtue and a community of love, it is an image of the loving communion of the Father, Son, and Holy Spirit. It is then an icon of the Trinity" *(USCCA, p. 377)*.

LET'S TALK >>>

- Ask your child to name some of the responsibilities of a bishop.
- Take turns sharing what you think would be the most interesting thing about being the Pope.

LET'S PRAY >>>

 Saint Gregory, pray for us that we may use our talents to serve others. Amen.

 For a multimedia glossary of Catholic Faith Words, Sunday readings, seasonal and Saint resources, and chapter activities go to **aliveinchrist.osv.com**.

Chapter 10 Review

A **Work with Words** Complete each sentence with the correct word or words from the Word Bank.

Word Bank

Holy Spirit

Apostolic

diocese

bishop

Magisterium

1. Many parishes make up a _____.

2. _____ Succession describes how the authority to lead and teach the Church was given to the Apostles and passed down to the bishops.

3. The _____ guides the Pope to lead the Church.

4. The _____ is the teaching office of the Church—all of the bishops in union with the Pope.

5. A _____ is an ordained man who teaches and leads members of the Church, making her holy.

B **Check Understanding** Match each description in Column A with the correct term in Column B.

Column A	Column B
6. head of the entire Catholic Church	Jesus
7. chose the Apostles to lead the Church	Pope
8. was the leader of the Apostles and first head of the Church	bishop
9. leads a diocese	Peter
10. leads a parish	pastor

Go to **aliveinchrist.osv.com** for an interactive review.

© Our Sunday Visitor

One and Holy

 ## Let Us Pray

Leader: Lord, God, you welcome all into your home. Help us to do your work.

"Unless the LORD build the house, they labor in vain who build." **Psalm 127:1**

All: Jesus, when we become one with you in Baptism, we become one with others in your Church. Let the Church be a sign of unity and welcome. Amen.

 ## God's Word

Jesus came and preached peace to everyone. So now, you are no longer strangers or wanderers. You are fellow citizens with the Saints and members of God's family. The Church is built upon the foundation of the Apostles and the prophets. Jesus is the center stone that holds everyone together. **Based on Ephesians 2:19–21**

What Do You Wonder?

- Could you really have the same courage as the Apostles?
- How can the Holy Spirit make us one?

United as One

How is the Catholic Church one?

Church communities are sometimes different, but all are one in Jesus. In other cultures, you would see some differences in the Mass celebration than what you would see in your own parish.

The same Mystery of Faith is being celebrated in all these places. The main parts of the Mass are the same everywhere because the Catholic Church is united as one.

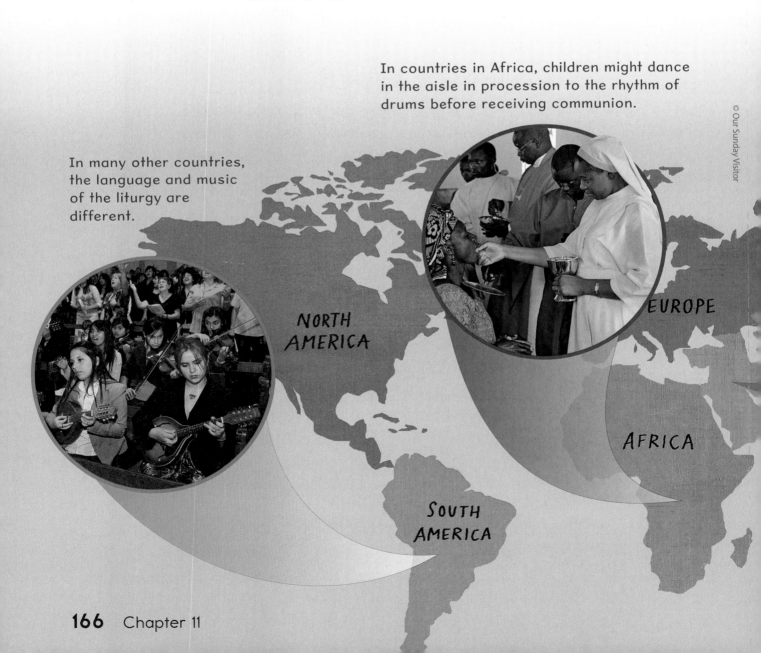

In countries in Africa, children might dance in the aisle in procession to the rhythm of drums before receiving communion.

In many other countries, the language and music of the liturgy are different.

NORTH AMERICA

EUROPE

AFRICA

SOUTH AMERICA

© Our Sunday Visitor

Identifying Characteristics

There are four **Marks of the Church**: **one**, **holy**, **catholic**, and **apostolic**. These Marks are linked together and show the essential features of the Church and her mission. The Church is one because the Holy Spirit unites members of the Church all over the world through one faith and one Baptism.

In India, a deacon might honor the Book of Gospels by passing a tray of fragrant flowers over it.

ASIA

AUSTRALIA

Catholic Faith Words

Marks of the Church the four characteristics that identify Christ's Church

one the Church is one because the power of the Holy Spirit unites all the members through one faith and one Baptism

holy the Church is holy because she is set apart for God and his purposes

catholic the Church is meant for all people in all times and all places

apostolic the teaching authority of the Church comes directly from Jesus and his chosen Apostles because the bishops of the Church are direct successors of the Apostles

Share Your Faith

Think How do you think Mass is celebrated in different parts of the world? Using a map or a globe, choose a country; then research how people celebrate Mass in that country.

Share Discuss with your group how Mass in that country might be different from Mass in the United States.

Fifty days after Jesus' Resurrection the Apostles were filled with the Holy Spirit at Pentecost.

Made Holy

What makes the Catholic Church holy?

People from many different countries were united when the Holy Spirit came to followers of Jesus on **Pentecost**. Pentecost marks the day the work of the Church began. From that day on, God's People understood more clearly that they were one body of believers who had been made holy.

© Our Sunday Visitor

Catholic Faith Words

Pentecost the feast that celebrates the coming of the Holy Spirit fifty days after Easter

Underline what happened to the Apostles when they were filled with the Holy Spirit at Pentecost.

 God's Word

The Coming of the Spirit

Fifty days after Jesus was raised from the dead, his followers were together in a house in Jerusalem. Suddenly, the house was filled with a noise like wind. Tongues of fire came to rest on each person in the room. All were filled with the Holy Spirit. They began speaking languages that they did not know.

Jerusalem was filled with Jews from all over the world that day. They heard the Apostles preaching. They were amazed that they could understand people from Galilee in their own languages. Based on Acts 2:1–12

Communion of Saints

The Holy Spirit continues to unify the Church today. The Spirit guides the leaders of the Church. The Spirit guides you to follow Jesus more closely and makes the Church holy.

Catholics all over the world are united by their faith in Christ. The Church is even united with the **Saints**, heroes of the Church who loved God, led holy lives, and are now in Heaven. The Church honors the Saints, especially Mary, the Mother of Jesus, for their holiness. Christians can learn from the examples of the Saints.

The Church is also called the **Communion of Saints**. This means that the members of the Church, both living and dead, form one Body in Christ. Even the Saints join you in worshipping the Father, the Son, and the Holy Spirit!

Catholic Faith Words

Saint a hero of the Church who loved God very much, led a holy life, and is now with God in Heaven

Communion of Saints everyone who believes in and follows Jesus—people on Earth and people who have died and are in Purgatory or in Heaven

Connect Your Faith

Name a Saint Write down the name of someone you know who belongs to the Communion of Saints.

_____

_____

belongs to the Communion of Saints.

Our Catholic Life

How do Saints help us live better?

The holy people of the past can teach you many things. From them, you can learn how to love God, lead a holy life, and make good choices. Saints are good examples and role models.

Look up the feast day for each Saint and write it under their names.

Saints

Saints are models or examples.
Someone who teaches you how to live is called a role model. Saints can show you how to love God and serve others.

We can turn to the Saints in prayer.
Because the Saints share God's life and love in Heaven, we can ask the Saints to pray for us and to help us know God's will.

Saints are patrons for jobs, people, and parishes.
Sometimes Saints are called patron Saints. This means that these Saints may have had particular jobs or talents that we share. People who have certain jobs or talents can look up to the Saints who had those same jobs and talents.

People named for Saints look to their name Saints for help.
If your parish church is named for a Saint, you can honor that Saint and ask him or her to pray for you to be a faithful follower of Jesus.

We remember the Saints' lives on their feast days.
At liturgies and celebrations, we learn more about the Saints and their holy actions.

- Saints Anne and Joachim

  Feast Day: _____

- Saint Katharine Drexel

  Feast Day: _____

- Saint Bede

  Feast Day: _____

- Saint Martin de Porres

  Feast Day: _____

People of Faith

Saints Perpetua and Felicity, died c. AD 202–203

March 7

Saints Perpetua and Felicity lived in Northern Africa. They died together for their faith. Perpetua was a rich woman who became a Christian. Felicity was a slave. She was a Christian, too. Both women had young children. Perpetua wrote about being in prison. She and Felicity helped each other be brave until they died. The Communion of Saints goes back to the start of the Church. In one of the prayers of the Mass, we remember many early Saints, like Perpetua and Felicity.

Discuss: Who are some of your favorite Saints?

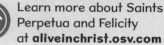

Learn more about Saints Perpetua and Felicity at **aliveinchrist.osv.com**

Live Your Faith

Illustrate a Holy Card Draw a picture of a Saint on the front of this holy card and write the Saint's name below your drawing. Then write a prayer on the back.

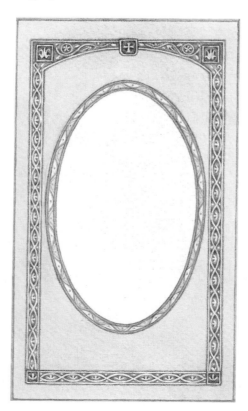

Amen

 **Let Us Pray**

Praying Together to the Holy Spirit

Gather and begin with the Sign of the Cross.
Children read their names and present their flowers.

Leader: So many people belong to the Communion of Saints.
Let us prayerfully name some. After every two names
we will pray:

All: Be with us in praising God the Father, God the Son, and
God the Holy Spirit.

Leader: Let us pray.

Bow your heads as the leader continues to pray.

All: Amen.

Offer one another a Sign of Peace.

Sing "Come to Us, Holy Spirit"
Come to us Holy Spirit
So we can know God's love
Come to us Holy Spirit
So we can know God's love
© 2010, Chet A. Chambers. Published
by Our Sunday Visitor.

YOUR CHILD LEARNED >>>

This chapter explains how the Holy Spirit continues to unify the Church and make her holy. One and holy are two Marks of the Church.

God's Word

 Read **Ephesians 2:19–21** and discuss how we are all members of God's family.

Catholics Believe

- The Marks of the Church are the four characteristics that identify Christ's Church: one, holy, catholic, and apostolic.

- The Communion of Saints includes all members of the Church, both living and dead, and form one Body in Christ.

To learn more, go to the *Catechism of the Catholic Church* #813, 814 at **usccb.org**.

People of Faith

This week, your child met Saints Perpetua and Felicity, early martyrs who are remembered in Eucharistic Prayer I.

CHILDREN AT THIS AGE >>>

How They Understand the Oneness of the Church To a third-grader, it might not seem like the Church is one at all. Children this age have often had friends and family that are part of other faith communities (or other parishes, if they are Catholic). It's important for them to know that Catholics are united through the Communion of Saints, by their faith in Jesus as God's Son, and by other core beliefs and practices.

CONSIDER THIS >>>

Have you ever wondered if you are speaking the same language as everyone else in the room?

People often hear what they want and not what is said. It might lead someone to wonder how the Church can speak clearly about God's revelation. "…the Holy Spirit, dwelling in the Church, draws the whole body of the faithful to believe what truly belongs to the faith. 'By this appreciation of the faith, aroused and sustained by the Spirit of truth, the People of God, guided by the sacred teaching authority (*magisterium*), and obeying it, receives not the mere word of men, but truly the word of God… (*LG, no. 12*)" (*USCCA, p. 25*).

LET'S TALK >>>

- Ask your child to name some differences between Mass at your parish and Mass in other parts of the world.

- Talk about all of the people in your family who are part of the Communion of Saints.

LET'S PRAY >>>

 Saints Perpetua and Felicity, we remember and honor you and ask you to pray for us now and at the hour of our death. Amen.

For a multimedia glossary of Catholic Faith Words, Sunday readings, seasonal and Saint resources, and chapter activities go to **aliveinchrist.osv.com**.

Chapter 11 Review

A **Work with Words** Match each description in Column A with the correct term in Column B.

Column A   Column B

1. unifies the   Jerusalem
   Church today

2. heroes of the Church   Saints
   who are with God in
   Heaven

3. another name   Pentecost
   for the Church

4. city where the   Holy Spirit
   Apostles received
   the Holy Spirit

5. celebrated fifty   Communion
   days after Easter   of Saints

B **Check Understanding** Fill in the circle beside the correct answer.

6. Pentecost celebrates the coming of the _____.
   ◯ New World   ◯ Holy Spirit

7. The Church honors the Saints, especially _____.
   ◯ Mary   ◯ the Pope

8. The main parts of the Mass are _____ around the world.
   ◯ the same   ◯ different

9. _____ unites Catholics all over the world.
   ◯ The music at Mass ◯ Faith in Jesus

10. You can learn how to _____ from studying the Saints.
   ◯ lead a holy life   ◯ pray

Go to **aliveinchrist.osv.com**
for an interactive review.

174 Chapter 11

Catholic and Apostolic

 Let Us Pray

Leader: Jesus, help us share your message.

"A report goes forth through all the earth, their messages, to the ends of the world." **Psalm 19:5**

All: We want to spread the Good News of your love with joy to all the world. Give us courage and fill us with desire. Amen.

God's Word

Let the word of Jesus live deeply in you. While you teach, remind one another of his ways. "And whatever you do, in word or in deed, do everything in the name of the Lord Jesus, giving thanks to God the Father through him." **Based on Colossians 3:16–17**

 What Do You Wonder?

- How can you bring the Good News of Jesus to others?
- Where are you supposed to bring the Good News of Jesus?

While on journeys and even from prison, Saint Paul wrote letters to new Christian communities.

A Man with a Mission

How did Saint Paul spread the Good News?

An important part of believing in Jesus is sharing his story. Saint Paul was one of the first people to share Jesus' story. This was his mission.

Paul's Mission

Circle the ways Saint Paul helped the early Church.

Saint Paul was one of the great Saints of the early Church. He traveled far from the Holy Land to preach about Jesus.

Wherever he traveled, Saint Paul tried to gather a group of people. He told them about Jesus. He helped them grow into a community. After staying with them for a while, Saint Paul would leave to tell others the Good News. The communities he left behind missed his guidance and would ask for his help even though he was far away.

Saint Paul wrote many letters to the groups he had started. He used the letters to answer questions, encourage them, and teach them even more about Jesus and his teachings. We still read the letters today. They are part of the Bible. We listen to them at Mass.

Sharing God's Good News

When he wrote, Saint Paul used many examples to explain his ideas. In this passage from a letter, he used the example of seeds and plants to show how the Church grew.

 God's Word

Doing God's Work

Who is Paul? Who is Apollos? We are ministers through whom you became believers. I planted the seed. My helper Apollos watered the seed. Then God made the seed grow. The planter and the waterer are not nearly as important as God is, because it is God who makes things grow. Apollos and I are God's coworkers. You are God's field. Based on 1 Corinthians 3:5–9

➡ **What was the seed that Saint Paul planted?**

Share Your Faith

Think Write one good work that you have done to help spread the Good News.

_____

_____

_____

Share In a small group, talk about how to help the seed of faith grow in others.

Universal and Missionary

How does the Church fulfill her mission?

© Our Sunday Visitor

Catholic Faith Words

evangelization sharing the Good News of Jesus through words and actions in a way that invites people to accept the Gospel

mission a job or purpose. The Church's mission is to announce the Good News of God's Kingdom.

missionaries people who answer God's call to bring the message of Jesus and announce the Good News of his Kingdom to people in other places

Saint Paul helped the early Christians know that the Church was for everyone. The Church is catholic because she is for all people in all times and places. The word catholic means "universal" or "everywhere."

The Church is apostolic because Jesus gave his Apostles the mission of sharing his Good News with people all over the world. This teaching authority has been passed on from the Apostles to their successors, the bishops. Jesus calls all of us to invite people to accept the Gospel by sharing the Good News with them. This work is called **evangelization**.

The Church's **mission**, or purpose, is to announce God's Kingdom. Mission can also mean a Church community in another country or in a remote place where people need to hear the Word of God.

Missionaries are people who answer God's call by traveling to bring Jesus' Good News to others, just as Paul did. You can help the Church's missionaries by praying for them and the people with whom they work. You can write letters to them and help raise money for things that the missionaries need.

Underline the things that missionaries do.

Missionaries travel the world and share the Good News with people in far away places.

Missionaries teach about Jesus and help people with their basic needs, such as a safe place to live.

Sharing with Others

Along with spreading the Good News of Jesus, missionaries also share food, shelter, medical supplies, and other things with the people who need their help. These things are important because they provide for people's basic needs. Christians have always shared with others and been concerned for their needs.

God wants you to share not only physical things, such as food, but also spiritual, or holy, things. That is why Christian missionaries teach people about Jesus and build churches, hospitals, and schools. They want people everywhere to hear God's Good News.

➜ **How can you share the Good News with other people?**

Connect Your Faith

Doing God's Work Find out who in your parish is serving God as a missionary. Write their name, location, and a sentence about what they are doing to spread the Good News.

_____

_____

One way we can help is to write letters to children our own age in our partner parish.

Our Catholic Life

How can partner parishes work together?

Sometimes a parish will have a special relationship with another parish. The two parishes may call each other "partner parishes" or "sister parishes." Here are some things that partner parishes do with and for each other.

Write one more suggestion that partner parishes can do to work together.

Partner Parishes

If the parishes are near each other, members of one parish sometimes attend Mass at the other parish; they also do activities together.

If the parishes are far apart, the members send letters, pray for one another, and sometimes exchange gifts.

If one of the parishes is a mission parish, the partner parish may send money, medicines, clothing, or send parishioners with useful skills to help the mission parish.

_____

_____

_____

People of Faith

Saint Elizabeth Ann Seton, 1774–1821

January 4

Saint Elizabeth Ann Seton is the first Saint who was born in the United States. She was married and had five children. After her husband died, Elizabeth became a Catholic. She wanted to do Jesus' work on Earth by serving others. She knew that people all over the world needed simple things. They need food, clothing, and to be able to go to school. She said that we must "live simply so that others may simply live." One of the things Saint Elizabeth did was open schools for poor children. She helped start the Catholic school system in the United States.

Discuss: How can you help do Jesus' work on Earth?

 Learn more about Saint Elizabeth Ann Seton at **aliveinchrist.osv.com**

Live Your Faith

Promote Your Parish What's special about your parish? Write, draw, or attach pictures of things that make your parish special.

 **Let Us Pray**

Prayer of Naming and Blessing

Gather and begin with the Sign of the Cross.

Leader: God, you have called us, your Church, to spread your goodness in the world. We take the time today to recall the times when we have seen others share your goodness.

As we plant seeds in our "planters," we will name a good work that we have seen or know is happening somewhere in the world. The seeds will remind us that there is someone sharing the Good News, somewhere the seeds of love and goodness are being planted.

Take turns planting seeds and mentioning good works.

Leader: As our seeds grow, they will remind us of our mission to plant the seeds of faith by praying and doing good works.

Bow your heads as the leader continues to pray.

All: Amen.

▶ Sing "Gathered as One"
Gathered as one, united we stand.
Your chosen people here in this land. Gathered to hear the Word of our God.
One Body alive in our faith.
© 2007, John Burland. All rights reserved.

FAMILY+FAITH
LIVING AND LEARNING TOGETHER

YOUR CHILD LEARNED >>>

This chapter covers the Marks of the Church: Catholic and Apostolic. The Church's mission is to share Jesus' Good News with the people of all nations.

God's Word

 Read **Colossians 3:16–17** to learn how the Word of Jesus can live in you.

Catholics Believe

- The Church's mission is to share Jesus' Good News with the people of all nations.
- The Church is catholic because she is everywhere and she welcomes everyone.

To learn more, go to the *Catechism of the Catholic Church* #830, 831 at **usccb.org**.

People of Faith

This week, your child met Saint Elizabeth Ann Seton, the first Saint born in the United States and the founder of the parochial school system. She said that we must "live simply so that others may simply live."

CHILDREN AT THIS AGE >>>

How They Understand the Mission of the Church People often ask children what they want to be when they grow up. The idea of a mission, either a personal or collective one, may not be familiar to children in third grade. Encourage them to consider what God is calling them to be. It's never too early for children to begin reflecting on this concept of God-given mission, especially as they begin to learn more about their talents and explore their interests.

CONSIDER THIS >>>

Have you ever been to Mass in another country or another state?

No matter where you are in the world, if you go to Mass you can be sure that every person that day is hearing the same Scripture proclaimed and receiving the real presence of Christ in the Eucharist. It is what we mean when we say we are one, catholic church. Although we are one, we express that diversity in many cultures. "The Catholic Church...continues to live in a diversity of cultures and languages because she is led by the Spirit of Christ to bring the Gospel to all peoples. She has known how to accept what is true and good in all cultures and...to infuse the truth and goodness of her tradition and life into them" (*USCCA, p. 129*).

LET'S TALK >>>

- Ask your child to name some ways he or she has shared Jesus' Good News with others.
- Talk about missionaries you have met and the countries they serve.

LET'S PRAY >>>

 God, bless and protect all missionaries throughout the world. Amen.

 For a multimedia glossary of Catholic Faith Words, Sunday readings, seasonal and Saint resources, and chapter activities go to **aliveinchrist.osv.com**.

Chapter 12 Review

A **Work with Words** Complete each sentence with the correct word from the Word Bank.

Word Bank

faith

churches

mission

sharing

apostolic

missionaries

1. The Church's _____ is to announce the Good News of God's Kingdom.

2. Jesus gave his Apostles the mission of _____ the Good News.

3. The Apostle Paul planted the seed of _____.

4. _____ bring Jesus' Good News of his Kingdom to people in other places.

5. Some missionaries help build _____, hospitals, and schools.

6. _____ means the teaching authority of the Church that comes directly from Jesus and his Apostles.

B **Check Understanding** Fill in the circle beside the correct answer.

7. Saint Paul shared the Good News by writing ____.
   ○ letters to new Christians   ○ a newspaper

8. The job of a missionary is to ____.
   ○ give money   ○ share Jesus' message

9. You can share in the mission of the Church by ____.
   ○ mailing letters   ○ sharing the Good News

10. The Church is called catholic because ____.
    ○ she is universal   ○ she is only for some

© Our Sunday Visitor

Go to **aliveinchrist.osv.com** for an interactive review.

A **Work with Words** Answer each question by writing the letter of the correct word from the Word Bank.

© Our Sunday Visitor

1. ☐ We travel to share Jesus' Good News. Who are we?

2. ☐ This feast celebrates the coming of the Holy Spirit. What is it?

3. ☐ We are the twelve men chosen by Jesus to be the leaders of his Church. Who are we?

4. ☐ We work with the Pope in teaching, guiding, and making the Church holy. Who are we?

5. ☐ This is a job or duty for which someone is responsible. What is it?

Word Bank

a. missionaries

b. Apostles

c. mission

d. Pentecost

e. bishops

B **Check Understanding** Circle the correct word to complete each sentence.

6. The name Peter means _____.

   rock   Church

7. The word bishop means _____.

   leader   overseer

8. The Pope is the bishop of _____.

   Italy   Rome

9. Saint _____ traveled on a mission to start new Christian communities.

   Paul   Peter

10. A bishop leads a _____.

    parish   diocese

Match each description in Column A with the correct term in Column B.

Column A	Column B
11. Everyone who believes in and follows Jesus Christ—on Earth, in Purgatory, and in Heaven	Magisterium
12. The four characteristics that identify Christ's Church	Communion of Saints
13. Leads a parish	Peter
14. Is the teaching office of the Church—all of the bishops in union with the Pope	evangelization
15. New name that Jesus gave to Simon	Marks of the Church

16.–20. Circle the words from the Word Bank in the word search.

```
D  G  K  T  C  S  S  C

D  D  X  Y  A  E  R  G

W  I  L  X  T  L  E  I

X  O  L  E  H  T  D  C

H  C  I  F  O  S  A  U

O  E  G  S  L  O  E  Q

E  S  D  D  I  P  L  L

U  E  F  H  C  A  Z  H
```

Word Bank

Catholic

diocese

Apostles

leaders

holy

C **Make Connections** Write a response to each question or statement on the lines below.

21. What is Apostolic Succession?

_____

_____

_____

22. How do the Saints help you grow in friendship with God?

_____

_____

23. Why is it important that the Church is united?

_____

_____

24. How could you use one of your talents to support the Church?

_____

_____

25. When have you noticed the Holy Spirit guiding you to follow Jesus?

_____

_____

Morality

Our Catholic Tradition

- The Beatitudes are teachings of Jesus that show the way to true happiness and tell how to live in God's Kingdom. (CCC, 1725)

- Jesus' New Commandment calls us to love and forgive one another as Jesus does. (CCC, 1985)

- We are lights to the world when we practice the Theological Virtues of faith, hope, and charity. (CCC, 1813)

- The Holy Spirit and Church teachings help us make good choices and avoid evil. (CCC, 2041)

How does God help you to make a good decision?

© Our Sunday Visitor

Choose Love

 ## Let Us Pray

Leader: Loving God, teach us to love as you love.

"The law of the LORD is perfect,
refreshing the soul." **Psalm 19:8**

All: Teach me to love as you love. Amen.

 ## God's Word

"But to you who hear I say, love your enemies, do good to those who hate you, bless those who curse you, pray for those who mistreat you.... Do to others as you would have them do to you." **Luke 6:27-28, 31**

? **What Do You Wonder?**

- Why should you love people who have done harm to you?

- How are you supposed to love like God?

Learning to Forgive

How did Joseph show forgiveness?

The Book of Genesis is the first book in the part of the Bible called the Old Testament. In it, we learn that God created human beings in his image and likeness. He gave us love and free will, which is the ability to choose.

During your life, you will have to make some hard choices. The following Scripture tells the story of a man who made a difficult choice after he was separated from his family. Joseph's story is found in the Old Testament.

Underline what Joseph's brothers did to him.

ⓣ God's Word

The Story of Joseph

Jacob was the father of twelve sons, but Joseph was his favorite. Joseph's brothers were jealous of him. They sold him to a group of travelers who made Joseph a slave.

Joseph became a slave in the faraway country of Egypt. He was given the important job of storing extra food because he was a hard worker and could

explain dreams. During this time, Joseph's family needed food because they were starving, so they traveled all the way to Egypt. Joseph's brothers did not recognize him because so many years had passed.

At first, Joseph did not tell them who he was. He was still angry with them.   Based on Genesis 37–45

Joseph chose to forgive his brothers because he loved them. Long before the time of Jesus, Joseph showed how to love those who hurt you.

➡ **How do you think Joseph's brothers felt when Joseph told them who he was?**

➡ **What other choices could Joseph have made?**

Share Your Faith

Think Have you ever had to forgive someone else without making a judgment?

Share Take turns sharing your thoughts with a partner.

The Way of Love

What does Jesus teach about love?

One day, Jesus was talking with his followers about how to treat people. This is what he told them.

Underline what Jesus wants us to do.

 God's Word

Love of Enemies

You have been told to love your friends and hate your enemies. But now I am telling you: Love your enemies, and pray for people who hurt you. This will make you children of God. God doesn't want you to do only what is easy. If you are friendly only to people who are friendly to you, why is that special? **Based on Matthew 5:43–47**

Jesus said that it is easier to love those who love you. He also said that you must love your enemies! That can be as difficult for people as it was for Joseph to forgive his brothers.

© Our Sunday Visitor

The New Commandment

Jesus' main teachings are about the love and care you are called to show God and others. In a teaching called the **Beatitudes**, Jesus said that those who make peace and show **mercy** are blessed by God. Jesus' **New Commandment** sums up the Ten Commandments and the Beatitudes in one statement: "…Love one another. As I have loved you, so you also should love one another" (John 13:34).

Living the New Commandment

People in your parish try to live by Jesus' New Commandment, too. There are probably volunteers who build houses, teach people to read, or give food to people who are hungry. They show their love by praying for and helping others. They show love by putting others' needs before their own.

Catholic Faith Words

Beatitudes teachings of Jesus that show the way to true happiness and tell how to live in God's Kingdom now and always

mercy kindness and concern for those who are suffering. God has mercy on us even though we are sinners.

New Commandment Jesus' command for his disciples to love one another as he has loved us

Connect Your Faith

Find the Message Solve the code by placing the correct letter in each blank to answer the question.

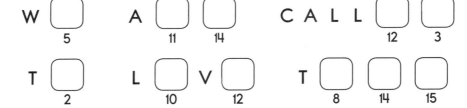

G	O	D		N	E	I	G	H	B	O	R		E	N	E	M	Y
1	2	3		4	5	6	7	8	9	10	11		12	13	14	15	16

What do these three words have in common?

W ☐(5)   A ☐(11) ☐(14)   C A L L ☐(12) ☐(3)

T ☐(2)   L ☐(10) V ☐(12)   T ☐(8) ☐(14) ☐(15)

Our Catholic Life

Why do we make the sign of peace?

There are many reasons that Catholics make the sign of peace during the Mass. Jesus told his followers to make peace with one another before they brought their gifts to the altar. The sign of peace is a way to obey Jesus' command.

Giving the sign of peace shows that the people gathered in the church are united as one community of believers.

God wants the whole world to live in peace. Remember to share a sign of peace with your family and neighbors. You get to know more people in your church family when you greet one another during the sign of peace.

Underline one way to obey Jesus' command.

People of Faith

Saint Peter Canisius, 1521–1597

December 21

Saint Peter Canisius lived when Protestants and Catholics were fighting each other. Peter knew that Jesus told us that we must love all people. We must even love people who are our enemies. Saint Peter wrote books explaining Catholic teaching. He said that we need to explain what we believe, but we must never be mean to people who don't believe the same things. Instead, we must listen to them and live with them in love. Saint Peter also loved Mary very much. He often prayed the Hail Mary.

Discuss: How can you love someone you don't like?

 Learn more about Saint Peter Canisius at **aliveinchrist.osv.com**

Live Your Faith

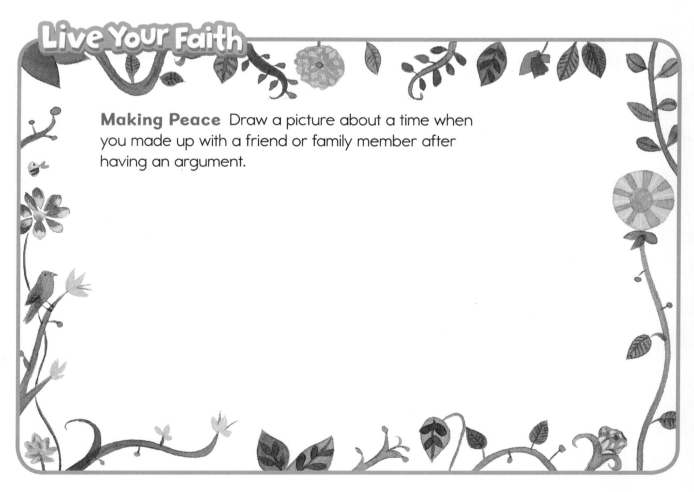

Making Peace Draw a picture about a time when you made up with a friend or family member after having an argument.

 **Let Us Pray**

Act of Love

Gather and begin with the Sign of the Cross.

Leader: God our Father, help us love as Jesus did.

Reader: When someone is mean to us, as Joseph's brothers were to him,

All: Help us forgive as Joseph did.

Reader: When we find it difficult to love,

All: Help us love as Jesus did.

Leader: We pray together an Act of Love.

All: O God, we love you above all things, with our whole heart and soul, because you are all-good and worthy of all love. We love our neighbor as ourselves for love of you. We forgive all who have injured us and ask pardon of all whom we have injured.

Leader: Let us pray.

Bow your heads as the leader prays.

All: Amen.

 Sing "Greatest Gift"
Love, love, Jesus is love.
God's greatest gift is the gift of love.
All creation sings together,
praising God for love.

FAMILY+FAITH
LIVING AND LEARNING TOGETHER

YOUR CHILD LEARNED >>>

This chapter describes the need to seek God's mercy and to ask for and offer forgiveness. It also focuses on Jesus' teachings to love others, especially our enemies.

God's Word

Read **Luke 6:27-31** and think about ways you can show your love for each family member.

Catholics Believe

- Jesus' New Commandment is to love one another as he loves each of us.
- The Beatitudes are teachings of Jesus that show the way to true happiness and tell how to live in God's Kingdom.

To learn more, go to the *Catechism of the Catholic Church* #1933, 1716 at **usccb.org**.

People of Faith

This week, your child met Saint Peter Canisius who urged us to always speak kindly to those with whom we disagree. He is credited with adding the sentence beginning, "Holy Mary, Mother of God" to the Hail Mary.

CHILDREN AT THIS AGE >>>

How They Understand the New Commandment Loving God above all things and loving others as God loves us may sound simple to a third-grader—until it comes to practical applications. We are often tested in these commands by the things we get most excited about or the people we are with every day. Your child will need many reminders of how he or she can apply these principles in daily life choices. For example, he or she might choose to go to church rather than staying home to play a video game or make a choice to not fight with a friend or sibling.

CONSIDER THIS >>>

How difficult is it to show kindness to someone who has harmed you?

Forgiveness may be the greatest challenge in our spiritual journey. It is sometimes difficult to imagine how people can let go of the resentment and bitterness they feel when they are wronged. Yet, "the best way to obtain mercy is to be merciful. As Jesus taught us, 'Blessed are the merciful, for they will be shown mercy' (Mt 5:7). Failure to forgive others is a major human problem. Holding grudges is common. Failure to forgive routinely tears apart families, neighborhoods, and even nations. Jesus stressed mercy and forgiveness in numerous ways" *(USCCA, p. 488)*.

LET'S TALK >>>

- Talk about a time when you've found it difficult to forgive. What did that experience teach you?
- Ask your child to name some times when he or she has asked forgiveness from someone else. How did it feel to receive that forgiveness?

LET'S PRAY >>>

 Holy Mary, Mother of God, pray for us sinners now and at the hour of our death. Amen.

 For a multimedia glossary of Catholic Faith Words, Sunday readings, seasonal and Saint resources, and chapter activities go to **aliveinchrist.osv.com**.

Chapter 13 Review

A **Work with Words** Match each description in Column A with the correct term in Column B.

Column A   Column B

1. Teachings of Jesus that show the way to true happiness   our enemies

2. Jesus' command to love others as he has loved us   love and forgiveness

3. A way to show that the people gathered in the church are one community of believers   Beatitudes

4. Jesus wants us to love   sign of peace

5. The story of Joseph is about this   New Commandment

B **Check Understanding** Put these events from the story of Joseph in order by numbering the sentences correctly.

6. ☐ Joseph recognizes his brothers, but they do not recognize him. Then Joseph tells his brothers who he is.

7. ☐ Joseph's father loves him very much. Joseph's brothers grow jealous.

8. ☐ Joseph forgives his brothers.

9. ☐ Joseph's brothers come to Egypt to ask for food.

10. ☐ Joseph's brothers sell him as a slave.

Go to **aliveinchrist.osv.com** for an interactive review.

Live in the Light

 Let Us Pray

Leader: God our Father, help us to be a light in the darkness.

"Send your light and your fidelity,
   that they may be my guide." Psalm 43:3

All: God, with you as our guide, we will learn how to love our neighbor. Amen.

God's Word

Jesus spoke to them again, saying, "I am the light of the world. Whoever follows me will not walk in darkness, but will have the light of life."

John 8:12

What Do You Wonder?

• Does your choice to shine the light of Jesus in the world really matter?

• How do you "practice" faith and hope?

The Light of the World

Who has shared the light of Christ with you?

Jesus talked about how people should help others find their way. He wanted to teach everyone how to glorify God. One day, Jesus told his followers what the world needed from them.

Underline what Jesus said others may see when you share your light.

 God's Word

Your Light Must Shine

"You are the light of the world," Jesus said. "A city set on a mountain cannot be hidden."

He went on, "Nor do they light a lamp and then put it under a bushel basket; it is set on a lampstand, where it gives light to all in the house."

Finally he said, "Just so, your light must shine before others, that they may see your good deeds and glorify your heavenly Father." Based on Matthew 5:14–16

We share Jesus' light during the Service of Light at Easter Vigil

Be a Light

Jesus taught about the many ways that we are called to show love and care for others. The good things you do for others show that you believe in God's Kingdom.

God's plan for your life is called your **vocation**. Each person has a purpose and our vocation helps us live that calling. When you choose loving actions, you are following God's plan. You are letting your light shine.

You are a light for the world when you help bring peace to others. Sometimes you work for peace in your own family and neighborhood. Sometimes you need to help people who live far away. Wherever help is needed, Jesus calls his followers to bring his peace.

Catholic Faith Words

vocation God's plan for our lives; the purpose for which he made us

Share Your Faith

Think Write one way you've been a light to others.

_____

_____

_____

Share With a group, discuss ways you have shared the light of Christ with someone.

The Virtues

How do the Theological Virtues help us?

Making good and loving choices helps you develop habits of goodness, called **virtues**. The word virtue means "strength." Practicing these good habits helps you make even more loving choices. The Theological Virtues come from God and help us to relate to him. We are first given these virtues in our Baptism.

The Theological Virtues

The **Theological Virtues** are faith, hope, and charity (love). They help to guide our relationship with the Holy Trinity.

Faith leads us to obey God. True faith is believing in God and all that he helps us understand about himself. As a follower of Jesus, you believe in him. Faith is both a gift from God and something we choose. Scripture tells us that real faith also produces good works.

© Our Sunday Visitor

Catholic Faith Words

virtues good spiritual habits that make you stronger and help you do what is right and good. They grow over time with our practice and openness to God's grace.

Theological Virtues the virtues of faith, hope, and charity (love), which are gifts from God that guide our relationship with him

faith the theological virtue that makes it possible for us to believe in God and all that he helps us understand about himself. Faith leads us to obey God.

Hope is the virtue that helps you trust in the true happiness that God the Father wants us to have. It helps us trust in Jesus' promises of eternal life, and to rely on the help of the Holy Spirit. As members of the Church, we hope for a world that is more like God's Kingdom.

Charity directs people to love God above all things and their neighbor as themselves. You show your love for God by helping people, loving others, and listening to friends who have problems. The Church helps you show love for God by teaching you how to treat everyone with kindness and respect.

In order to get better at something, you need to practice. You have to practice virtues. When you do, these gifts from God—faith, hope, and charity—grow strong in you.

Catholic Faith Words

hope the Theological Virtue that helps us trust in the true happiness God wants us to have and in Jesus' promises of eternal life, and to rely on the help of the Holy Spirit

charity the Theological Virtue of love. It directs us to love God above all things and our neighbor as ourselves, for the love of God.

Connect Your Faith

Create a Reminder Design and decorate a bookmark about practicing one of the virtues as you share the light of Christ with others.

Our Catholic Life

How can you make prayer a part of your day?

The virtues of faith, hope, and charity help you develop your prayer life.

- **Prayers of faith** show God that you believe in him.

- **Prayers of hope** tell God that you trust in him, even when times are tough.

- **Prayers of charity** (love) show God that you love him and will show your love to others by being kind.

There are many ways to add prayer to your day. If you aren't already saying morning prayers, mealtime prayers, and bedtime prayers, you can easily develop the habit of praying at these times. Some families say prayers at special times, such as before leaving on a trip. Talk to your family about adding more prayer to your lives.

© Our Sunday Visitor

Place a check mark next to the times you pray during the day.

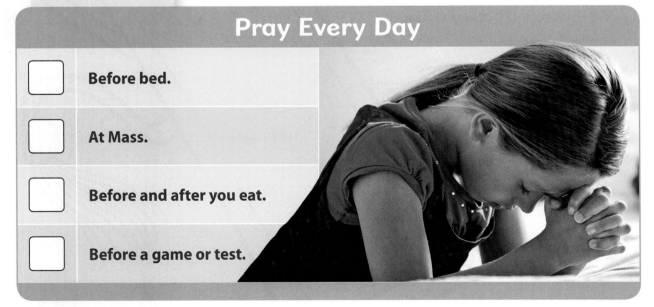

Pray Every Day

- [ ] **Before bed.**
- [ ] **At Mass.**
- [ ] **Before and after you eat.**
- [ ] **Before a game or test.**

People of Faith

Saint Genevieve, c. 422–500

January 3

Saint Genevieve lived in France. When she was young, she decided that she wanted to share the light of Christ with everyone she met. She lived the virtues her whole life and showed her faith by praying. Attila the Hun and his army didn't attack Paris because Saint Genevieve led the people in prayer. She showed her hope by building a church that people still use. She gave food to hungry people and asked the King to have mercy on prisoners. Saint Genevieve often wore a crucifix to remind her to think about Jesus.

Discuss: When have you helped others in need?

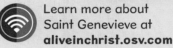

Learn more about Saint Genevieve at **aliveinchrist.osv.com**

Live Your Faith

Remember to Pray With a group, list several times of day when you can pray. Make a list of ways to remind yourself to pray.

When to Pray:

_____

_____

_____

_____

_____

_____

Reminders to Pray:

_____

_____

_____

_____

_____

_____

 **Let Us Pray**

Prayer of Petition

Gather and begin with the Sign of the Cross.

Leader: We pray together, asking Jesus to help us grow in faith, hope, and charity.

All: We know you, and so we have faith in you, O Jesus.

Reader 1: Help us act with love toward one another.

Reader 2: Help us share the light of your love.

Reader 3: Give us the hope of living with you in Heaven.

All: Amen.

Leader: Let us pray.

Bow your heads as the leader prays.

All: Amen.

 Sing "Share the Light"
Share the light of Jesus.
Share the light that shows the way.
Share the light of Jesus.
Share God's spirit today. Share God's spirit today.
Repeat Verse

Share the word…
Share the love…
Share the smile...
Share the light…

FAMILY + FAITH
LIVING AND LEARNING TOGETHER

YOUR CHILD LEARNED >>>

This chapter explores the importance of sharing Christ's light with others and the Theological Virtues of faith, hope, and charity (love).

God's Word

 Read **John 8:12** to learn how you can help others to see Jesus' light.

Catholics Believe

- Each of us has a purpose and vocation that helps us follow God's plan and be a light to the world.
- God's gifts of faith, hope, and charity (love) help you live a good and moral life.

To learn more, go to the *Catechism of the Catholic Church* #1813, 1877 at **usccb.org**.

People of Faith

This week, your child met Saint Genevieve, the patron Saint of Paris. She is said to have thwarted the attack of Attila the Hun through prayer.

CHILDREN AT THIS AGE >>>

How They Understand Sharing the Light of Christ It's a powerful feeling for children when they realize they can have an impact on others. Your child can do this in both positive and negative ways. Particularly if he or she has younger siblings at home, but also with peers and even people who are older, your child can spread the light of Christ through kind actions and virtuous example. This will usually mean something different for each child, but third graders often need to be reminded that they serve as examples for others.

CONSIDER THIS >>>

How quick are you to recognize the bad habits of yourself or others?

It is easy to see other's bad habits. We are familiar with our own as well—so much so that it may be easier to name our bad habits than recognize our good ones. "[Virtues] are acquired by frequent repetition of virtuous acts that establish a pattern of virtuous behavior.... Yet it is through doing good acts in the concrete that the virtue within us is strengthened and grows" *(USCCA, p. 317).*

LET'S TALK >>>

- Talk about a time when your trust in God has given you hope.
- Ask your child to name some good habits that he or she has.

LET'S PRAY >>>

 Saint Genevieve, help us to be the light of Christ and share God's love with all we meet. Amen.

 For a multimedia glossary of Catholic Faith Words, Sunday readings, seasonal and Saint resources, and chapter activities go to **aliveinchrist.osv.com**.

A **Work with Words** Complete Jesus' message with the correct words from the Word Bank.

1–5. Jesus said, "You are the _____.

A city on a mountaintop cannot be

_____. Your light must

_____ before others, that they may

see your good _____ and glorify

your Heavenly _____."

B **Check Understanding** Match each description in Column A with the correct term in Column B.

Column A	Column B
6. Helps you trust in God's promise of happiness and Jesus' promise of eternal life.	faith
7. Helps you believe in God and all that he has made known to us.	charity
8. You can do this at any time of day, not just at meals or bedtime.	virtues
9. Helps us love God and our neighbor.	pray
10. Good spiritual habits that make you stronger and help you choose right.	hope

Go to **aliveinchrist.osv.com** for an interactive review.

Help with Choices

 ## Let Us Pray

Leader: God, help me to follow you.

"Guide me by your fidelity and teach me,
for you are God my savior." Psalm 25:5

All: Jesus, help me to listen for the voice of the Holy
Spirit in your Word and in the Church so that I
may choose what is right. Amen.

 ## God's Word

Look deep into my heart, O God. You know
my deepest thoughts. See if I am going in the
wrong direction, then lead me back to you.
Based on Psalm 139:23–24

? What Do You Wonder?

- Is God mad when you do
something wrong?

- Who do you trust to help you
learn what is right and wrong?

Many Choices

How do you make good choices?

Your life is full of choices. Some don't make much of a difference, such as which color of shirt you wear on a Saturday.

Some choices do make a big difference, though. Sometimes you must choose between a bad thing and a good thing. If you are lucky, the choice is easy. Sometimes, the choice can be difficult.

Everyone needs help to make good choices. The Holy Spirit helps you. God's free and loving gift of **grace** in the Sacraments can help you. Parents, priests, and teachers can help you prepare for choices by giving you guidance and helping you form your **conscience**. God gave you your conscience to help you choose between right and wrong.

➤ Why are some choices harder to make than others?

➤ What do you do when you have a choice to make?

Catholic Faith Words

grace God's free and loving gift to humans of his own life and help

conscience an abiltiy given to us by God that helps us make choices about right and wrong

Precepts of the Church some of the minimum requirements given by Church leaders for deepening our relationship with God and the Church

© Our Sunday Visitor

The Church Guides Choices

The Church helps us make good choices, too. We use the teachings of the Church to guide our choices. The Church teaches us to follow the Ten Commandments and the Beatitudes. The Church tells us we must also follow its basic requirements, the **Precepts of the Church**, in order to deepen our relationship with God and the Church.

Precepts of the Church

Precept	How Each Precept Guides You
1. Take part in Mass on Sundays and Holy Days of Obligation. Keep these days holy and avoid unnecessary work.	Makes sure that you take time to be with Jesus and your parish community, strengthens your faith, rests your body, and encourages you to enjoy the world God has given you
2. Celebrate the Sacrament of Penance and Reconciliation at least once a year if there is serious sin.	Helps you look at your life to see how you need God's forgiveness and which actions you need to improve
3. Receive Holy Communion at least once a year during Easter time.	Strengthens your faith and makes you one with Jesus
4. Fast and abstain on days of penance.	Helps you share in the sacrifice of Jesus, train yourself spiritually, and experience the hunger of people who are poor
5. Give your time, gifts, and money to support the Church.	Encourages you to support the Church and participate in her works

Share Your Faith

Think Pick out one of the Precepts. How does it help Catholics become holy?

Share Share your answer with a partner and talk about why the precepts are important.

Changing Directions

How do you overcome making a bad choice?

What happens when someone makes bad choices? This Scripture story shows how someone who made bad choices can change.

Underline what the voice said to Saul.

 **God's Word**

Saul and Jesus

Shortly after his Resurrection, Jesus returned to his Father in Heaven. A man named Saul began turning in followers of Jesus to the authorities.

One day, Saul was traveling between towns. A bright light flashed around him. He heard a voice say, "Saul, Saul, why are you persecuting me?"

Saul asked, "Who are you?"

The voice answered, "I am Jesus … go into the city and you will be told what you must do."

Saul did as Jesus said. He was baptized and became a great Christian preacher and writer. He is now known as Saint Paul, his new name in Christ.

Based on Acts 9:1–30

The Sacrament of Penance and Reconciliation

Like Saul, everyone makes wrong choices at times. The choice to disobey God on purpose is called **sin**. When you sin, you hurt your relationship with God and other people. But there are things you can do to help make things right again.

You can experience God's forgiveness in the Sacrament of Penance and Reconciliation, also called confession. Through this Sacrament, God gives you a chance to take these actions through his Church:

- Look at what you have done.

- Say you are sorry, seek forgiveness, and receive absolution.

- Repair or make up for the wrong you have done, and change your behavior.

© Our Sunday Visitor

Catholic Faith Words

sin a person's choice to disobey God on purpose and do what he or she knows is wrong. Sins hurt our relationship with God and other people.

Connect Your Faith

Talk It Over With a partner, talk about making good choices in the following situation, and list your choices in the space below.

You can see your best friend's test paper from where you are sitting, and you know that she always gets the highest grade.

_____

_____

_____

213

Our Catholic Life

How do you tell right from wrong?

You know that your conscience guides you in making right decisions. It is up to you to learn what is right and wrong so that you can use that knowledge when you need to make a choice. Information about what is right and wrong can be found in many different places.

Write the first words of each step in order below.

Form Your Conscience

- **Pray** to the Holy Spirit, asking for help to make a right choice.
- **Learn** the Ten Commandments, the Beatitudes, and the Precepts of the Church.
- **Listen** to the homily at Mass, and pay attention during religion lessons to learn God's laws.
- **Ask** a parent or another trusted adult.
- **Receive** the Sacraments, and be strengthened to follow God's will.

1. _____

2. _____

3. _____

4. _____

5. _____

People of Faith

Saint Pio (Padre Pio), 1887–1968

September 23

Saint Padre Pio was born in Italy. His parents were farmers. At age 15, he began studying to become a Capuchin priest. He took the name Pio in honor of Pope Saint Pius V. Padre Pio knew that confession was very important. He said that going to confession was like dusting the soul. He heard the confessions of people who traveled from all over. He helped them feel God's mercy and forgiveness. Padre Pio was known for having the stigmata, the visible wounds of Christ. He would tell people "Pray, hope, and don't worry."

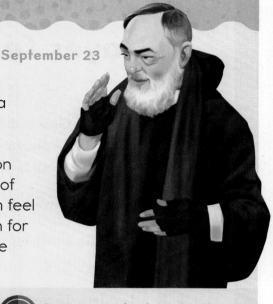

Discuss: When have you felt God's mercy?

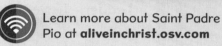 Learn more about Saint Padre Pio at **aliveinchrist.osv.com**

Live Your Faith

The Path of Conscience With a partner, flip a coin to move along the path. Heads moves one space; tails moves two spaces. The first player to finish is the winner.

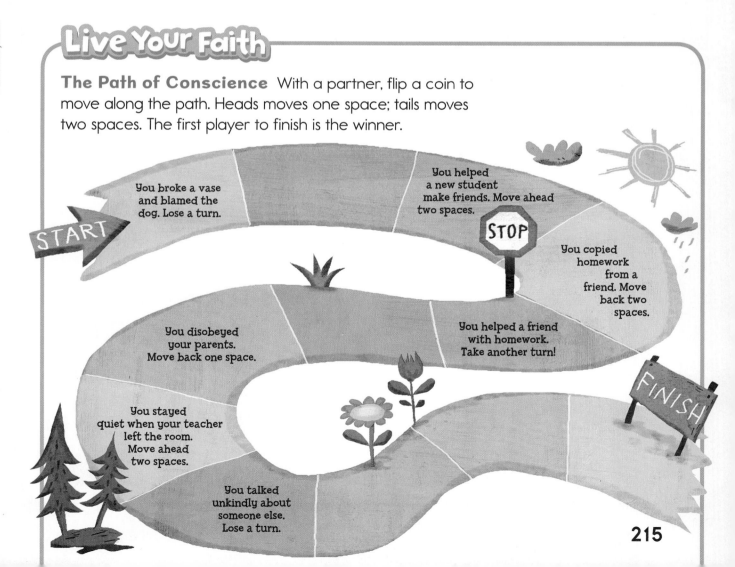

START

You broke a vase and blamed the dog. Lose a turn.

You helped a new student make friends. Move ahead two spaces.

STOP

You copied homework from a friend. Move back two spaces.

You disobeyed your parents. Move back one space.

You helped a friend with homework. Take another turn!

You stayed quiet when your teacher left the room. Move ahead two spaces.

You talked unkindly about someone else. Lose a turn.

FINISH

 **Let Us Pray**

Prayer for Forgiveness

Gather and begin with the Sign of the Cross.

Leader: God our Loving Father, we come to you to ask forgiveness. Sometimes we have not behaved as we should.

Leader: If we have quarreled and called each other names,

All: Lord, let your mercy be on us, as we place our trust in you.

Leader: If we are lazy at home and in school,

All: Lord, let your mercy be on us, as we place our trust in you.

Leader: If we have not done good for others when we had the chance,

All: Lord, let your mercy be on us, as we place our trust in you.

Leader: Let us pray.

Bow your heads as the leader prays.

All: Amen.
Based on the *Rite of Penance.*

 Sing "God of Mercy"

FAMILY+FAITH
LIVING AND LEARNING TOGETHER

YOUR CHILD LEARNED >>>

This chapter explains how grace, conscience, and the Precepts of the Church help us follow God and make good choices.

God's Word

 Read **Psalm 139:23–24** and discuss how God leads you in the right direction.

Catholics Believe

- Conscience is the ability given to us by God that helps us make choices about right and wrong.

- God's grace in the Sacraments, and the Holy Spirit, help us make changes and good choices.

To learn more, go to the *Catechism of the Catholic Church* #1777, 1785 at **usccb.org**.

People of Faith

This week, your child met Saint Padre Pio. He said that regular confession was one of the keys to a holy life.

CHILDREN AT THIS AGE >>>

How They Understand Making Good Choices Third graders often define good choices in terms of the parameters they have been given by people they trust. These parameters are often specific to place or situation. Because children this age depend a great deal on social expectations, it's important that this early conscience formation occur in family environments that are trustworthy and supportive of Catholic moral values.

CONSIDER THIS >>>

Who in your life do you trust to give you good advice?

We are careful about who we trust to give us advice. We realize that even those we trust can be wrong because of our limitedness as human beings. "Wisdom enables us to see the world from God's viewpoint, which can help us come to grasp the purpose and plan of God. It grants us the long-range view of history, examining the present in the light of the past and the mystery of the future. It saves us from the illusion that the spirit of the times is our only guide" (*USCCA, p. 208*).

LET'S TALK >>>

- Ask your child to name one of the actions he or she can do to experience God's forgiveness.

- Talk about how you've experienced God's forgiveness in the Sacrament of Penance and Reconciliation.

LET'S PRAY >>>

 Saint Pio, pray for us that we may learn to turn to God often for forgiveness and mercy. Amen.

 For a multimedia glossary of Catholic Faith Words, Sunday readings, seasonal and Saint resources, and chapter activities go to **aliveinchrist.osv.com**.

Chapter 15 Review

A **Work with Words** Fill in the circle beside the correct answer.

1. Your conscience is a _____ in making good decisions.
   ○ prayer   ○ guide   ○ sin

2. A sin is a(n) _____ to disobey God.
   ○ deliberate choice   ○ accident   ○ mistake

3. God's free and loving gift to us of his own life and help is called _____.
   ○ spirit   ○ grace   ○ words

4. The _____ of the Church are some of the minimum requirements for deepening our relationship with God and the Church.
   ○ laws   ○ liturgy   ○ Precepts

5. The Church offers God's _____ in the Sacrament of Penance and Reconciliation.
   ○ anger   ○ forgiveness   ○ conscience

B **Check Understanding** Write responses on the lines below.

6. Whose voice did Saul hear? _____

7. What did Saul do after he heard the voice?

   _____

8. What new name did Jesus give to Saul? _____

9. Why do you need to form your conscience?

   _____

10. What can help you form your conscience?

    _____

Go to **aliveinchrist.osv.com** for an interactive review.

A Work with Words Match each description in Column A with the correct term in Column B.

Column A	Column B
1. An ability given to us by God that helps us make choices about right and wrong	Beatitudes
2. Teachings of Jesus that show the way to true happiness	virtues
3. Basic duties of Catholics	Precepts of the Church
4. Good spiritual habits that help you choose right	New Commandment
5. Jesus' command to love others as he loves us	conscience

Write the letter T if the sentence is TRUE. Write the letter F if the sentence is False.

6. [ ] Catholics should receive Holy Communion at least once a year.

7. [ ] Charity (love) means believing in God.

8. [ ] Theological Virtues are a gift from God.

9. [ ] The Precepts of the Church are minimum requirements for deepening our relationship with God and the Church.

10. [ ] Jesus wants us to hold grudges against others.

B **Check Understanding** Complete each sentence by circling the correct word.

11. You can experience God's forgiveness in the Sacrament of _____.

    Penance and Reconciliation   **Baptism**

12. Jesus said, "You are the _____ of the world."

    leader   **light**

13. When you sin, you hurt your relationship with _____.

    yourself   **God**

14. _____ was sold by his brothers into slavery.

    Joseph   **Paul**

15. After his Baptism, Saul became known as _____.

    Paul   **Simon**

Write responses on the lines below. What are the five Precepts of the Church?

16–20. _____

_____

_____

_____

_____

_____

_____

C **Make Connections** Write responses on the lines below.

21. How do you show your faith?

_____

_____

22. What did the story of Joseph and his brothers teach you about forgiveness?

_____

_____

23. List two of the Beatitudes and what you have done to follow them.

_____

_____

24. Give an example of the difference between sinning and making a mistake.

_____

_____

25. How do you follow Jesus' New Commandment?

_____

_____

_____

Sacraments

Our Catholic Tradition

- The three Sacraments of Initiation celebrate membership into the Church: Baptism, Confirmation, and Eucharist. (CCC, 1212)

- The Sacraments of Healing help people in need of forgiveness and healing during times of physical and spiritual sickness. (CCC, 1421)

- The Sacraments at the Service of Communion celebrate people's commitment to serve God and the community. (CCC, 1534)

Why are the symbols, words, and actions of the Seven Sacraments important in our worship?

Bishops receive the authority to lead, teach, and make holy the Church.

© Our Sunday Visitor

Sacraments of Initiation

♥ Let Us Pray

Leader: Loving God, help us answer your call.

"Sing to the LORD a new song,
his praise in the assembly of the
faithful." **Psalm 149:1**

All: In Baptism, we receive your call to grow in
holiness. We ask you, Jesus, to give us the eyes to
see the many ways we can grow deeper in love
with you. Amen.

✝ God's Word

Peter wrote a letter to the Christians in the early Church. He told them, "You are a people chosen by God, a people who serve and worship God. You give praise to Jesus for he called you out of darkness into his wonderful light. Once you were not a family, but now you are God's family. You had not received mercy, but now you have received mercy." **Based on 1 Peter 2:9–10**

❓ What Do You Wonder?

- How are you chosen by God?
- Why did your parents want you to be baptized?

New Life in God

How does someone become a member of the Catholic Church?

Most people receive new life in God and become members of the Catholic Church when they are baptized as babies. This story is about an adult who found new life in Christ.

New Life Begins

Steve's family was watching a video of the Easter Vigil celebration. Aunt Kim and the other adults had celebrated three Sacraments in one evening. First, they were baptized. Then, they were confirmed with the anointing of **Sacred Chrism**. Finally, they received Holy Communion.

After Mass, everyone was laughing and hugging Aunt Kim and the others. Steve enjoyed all the excitement. He looked very happy on the video!

Catholic Faith Words

Sacred Chrism perfumed oil used for anointing in the Sacraments of Baptism, Confirmation, and Holy Orders

Underline the three things that took place when Aunt Kim received three Sacraments in one celebration.

Life in the Church

After they saw the video, the family looked at photos. "Look, Steve," his sister Laura said. "Here are pictures of your Baptism. And here you are on your First Communion day."

The family noticed some differences between the celebrations. Baby Steve wore a white baptismal gown, but Aunt Kim wore a brown robe before her Baptism and changed into a white one after. Steve received First Communion in second grade. Kim was an adult, and she received the Eucharist on the same day she was baptized.

Still, some things were the same. Steve's godfather was Aunt Kim's sponsor, too. Father John had baptized both Steve and Aunt Kim.

Aunt Kim celebrated three Sacraments at the Easter Vigil. Sacraments are signs that come from Jesus. Through the power of the Holy Spirit, Jesus works in and through the Sacraments to give grace, a share in God's life and work.

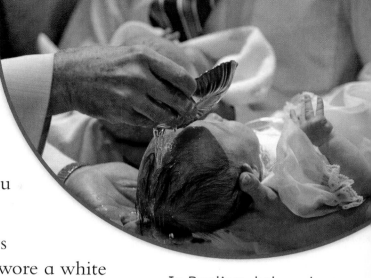

In Baptism, holy water is poured over the person's head or the person is immersed in water three times, in the name of the Holy Trinity.

→ **What do you remember most from a First Communion celebration that you've seen?**

Share Your Faith

Think Draw a picture to illustrate how your parish celebrates First Communions.

Share your drawing with a small group.

Church Membership
What are the Sacraments of Initiation?

From the beginning of the Church, the **Sacraments of Initiation** have been an important and necessary part of our faith. Baptism is the first Sacrament we receive. It leads to the other Sacraments of Initiation: Confirmation and **Eucharist**. Listen to Peter speak about Baptism to a crowd of people who did not know about Jesus.

Catholic Faith Words

Sacraments of Initiation the three Sacraments that celebrate membership into the Catholic Church: Baptism, Confirmation, and Eucharist

Eucharist the Sacrament in which Jesus shares himself, and the bread and wine become his Body and Blood

Real Presence the teaching that Jesus is really and truly with us in the Eucharist. We receive Jesus in his fullness.

 ## God's Word

Many Are Baptized

On Pentecost, Peter said to the crowd, "Repent and be baptized, every one of you, in the name of Jesus Christ for the forgiveness of your sins; and you will receive the gift of the holy Spirit."

Peter told the people that Jesus' promise was meant for everyone. Many of them accepted his message. About 3,000 people were baptized that day. **Based on Acts 2:38–41**

Receiving and Sharing God's Love

In each of the Sacraments of Initiation, you see the actions and hear the words of the minister, who acts in the name of the Holy Trinity. Jesus, the Son, by the power of the Holy Spirit, shares with you the love of the Father. In the Sacrament of the Eucharist we honor Christ's **Real Presence** and receive him in Holy Communion.

Underline important words we hear in each Sacrament.

Sacraments of Initiation

	Words and Actions	Effects
 **Baptism**	The priest or deacon pours water on or immerses the person, saying, "I baptize you in the name of the Father, and of the Son, and of the Holy Spirit."	Removes Original Sin, forgives personal sin, and gives new life in Christ; marks the person as a member of Christ's Body, the Church; unites all Christians
 **Confirmation**	The bishop or priest lays hands on the person's head and then anoints him or her with Sacred Chrism, saying, "Be sealed with the Gift of the Holy Spirit."	Seals and completes Baptism; strengthens the person's bond with the Church; unites the person more fully with Christ; strengthens him or her in living the faith
 **Eucharist**	The priest prays the Eucharistic Prayer, consecrating bread and wine, saying "This is my Body, which will be given up for you.…This is the chalice of my blood… shed for you and for many." Then he shares Christ's Body and Blood with the Church community.	Brings forgiveness of venial sins and an increase of grace; unites all who share the Eucharist into the one Body of Christ

Connect Your Faith

Show Welcome Write one way your Church family welcomes a new member.

_____

_____

Our Catholic Life

How can you help welcome new members into the Catholic Church?

When a good friend or relative visits your family, or when a baby brother or sister joins your family, you welcome that person. You might have a party. You might make a sign that says "Welcome!" You might show a visitor where to sit at the dinner table.

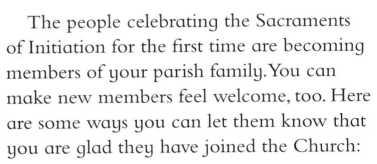

The people celebrating the Sacraments of Initiation for the first time are becoming members of your parish family. You can make new members feel welcome, too. Here are some ways you can let them know that you are glad they have joined the Church:

- In some parishes, babies are baptized at a Sunday Mass. If you are present during one of these celebrations, pay close attention and pray for those being baptized.

- Every year at the Easter Vigil, people join the Catholic Church. They receive the Sacraments of Christian Initiation. Pray for those joining the Church. As a class project, create "Welcome to the Church" cards for them.

- First Communions and Confirmations take place as part of parish life, too. Ask a parish leader for a list of those preparing to receive these Sacraments. Select one name and pray for that person.

➡ **What makes you feel welcome in your parish?**

People of Faith

Saint John the Baptist, first century

June 24

Saint John the Baptist was Jesus' cousin. An angel came to Saint John's father, Zechariah, to say that he and his wife Elizabeth would have a baby. Mary, the Mother of Jesus, visited Elizabeth when she was pregnant. John grew up to be a preacher. He prepared the way for Jesus by telling people the Good News that God would come to save his People. When Jesus was ready to start his ministry, Saint John baptized him in the River Jordan. Saint John was killed for pointing out the bad things that King Herod was doing.

Discuss: Talk about a Baptism that you have seen. Who was baptized? What happened?

Learn more about Saint John the Baptist at **aliveinchrist.osv.com**

Live Your Faith

Helped You Feel Welcome Write your name and the names of three people in your parish who have helped you feel welcome.

_____ _____ _____ _____

 **Let Us Pray**

Pray with God's Word

Gather and begin with the Sign of the Cross.

Reader 1: A reading from the Gospel according to Mark.

Read Mark 1:9–11.

Reader 2: Jesus went to the Jordan River from Nazareth.

Reader 3: He was baptized by John.

Reader 1: When he came out of the water, the Holy Spirit came down from the sky in the form of a dove.

Leader: Let us pray.

Bow your head as the leader prays.

All: Amen.

 Sing "The Seven Sacraments"
The Sacraments, the Seven Sacraments.
Signs that come from Jesus and give us grace.
The Sacraments, the Seven Sacraments.
Signs that God is with us in a special way.
© 2008, John Burland. All rights reserved.

FAMILY+FAITH

LIVING AND LEARNING TOGETHER

YOUR CHILD LEARNED >>>

This chapter discusses the words and actions of the Sacraments of Initiation which celebrate membership into the Catholic Church: Baptism, Confirmation, and Eucharist.

God's Word

 Read **1 Peter 2:9–10** to read how we are all part of God's family.

Catholics Believe

- Baptism removes Original Sin, forgives personal sin, and gives new life in Christ. Confirmation seals and completes Baptism.

- In the Eucharist, Jesus shares himself with us, giving us the gift of his Body and Blood.

To learn more, go to the *Catechism of the Catholic Church* #1212, 1271, 1323 at **usccb.org**.

People of Faith

This week, your child met Saint John the Baptist who baptized Jesus. Share pictures from your own family Baptisms.

CHILDREN AT THIS AGE >>>

How They Understand the Sacraments of Initiation

Because third-graders are just beginning to form social groups and understand what it means to belong to a community, this is an ideal time for your child to understand the Sacraments of Initiation as the way in which one enters the Church community. While many third-graders will not remember their Baptism, most of them will have celebrated another Sacrament of Christian Initiation, Eucharist, for the first time just last year. Their continued celebration of Eucharist reinforces their participation at the family table.

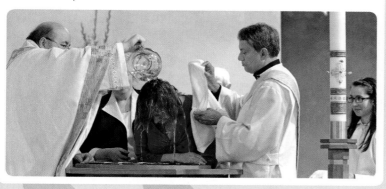

CONSIDER THIS >>>

Do you think of your Baptism as an event, or the beginning of a relationship?

While many of us think of Baptism as a happy event that happened in our lives or the lives of our children, we often do not see it as a moment that began a life of relationship, much like a wedding. Baptism sets us on a lifetime journey of growing ever more deeply in our knowledge and love of Jesus Christ. "In Baptism, the Holy Spirit moves us to answer Christ's call to holiness. In Baptism, we are asked to walk by the light of Christ and to trust in his wisdom. We are invited to submit our hearts to Christ with ever deeper love" *(USCCA p. 196).*

LET'S TALK >>>

- Talk about the ways that your family celebrates new beginnings.

- Ask your child to name some ways he or she can welcome new members of the Church.

LET'S PRAY >>>

 John the Baptist, pray for us, that we may continue to live the faith we received at Baptism and share that faith with others. Amen.

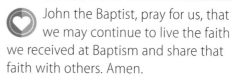 For a multimedia glossary of Catholic Faith Words, Sunday readings, seasonal and Saint resources, and chapter activities go to **aliveinchrist.osv.com**.

Chapter 16 Review

A **Work with Words** Fill in the circle beside the correct answer.

1. _____ is the perfumed oil used in some Sacraments.

   ○ Eucharist   ○ Baptism   ○ Sacred Chrism

2. Baptism, Holy Eucharist, and Confirmation are all Sacraments of _____.

   ○ Initiation   ○ Childhood   ○ Holiness

3. Initiation is a word that means _____.

   ○ faith   ○ beginning   ○ Church

4. Holy Eucharist brings _____.

   ○ resolution   ○ Sainthood   ○ unity with Christ

5. Confirmation strengthens your bond with _____.

   ○ your parents   ○ the Church   ○ yourself

B **Check Understanding** Match each description in Column A with the correct term in Column B.

Column A	Column B
6. Removes Original Sin	Sacraments
7. Signs that come from Jesus and give grace	Sacraments of Initiation
8. Catholics receive the Body and Blood of Christ	Baptism
9. Celebrates membership into the Catholic Church	Confirmation
10. Seals and completes Baptism	Eucharist

© Our Sunday Visitor

Go to **aliveinchrist.osv.com** for an interactive review.

Sacraments of Healing

 Let Us Pray

Leader: O God, give me strength.

"O LORD, my God,
 I cried out to you for help and you
 healed me." Psalm 30:3

All: Son of God, you comforted those you met as you taught and traveled. So many people are sick today. Bless them, Jesus, and help them to know that you are there with them. Amen.

 God's Word

After crossing the sea, Jesus and his disciples came to a small town. When the men of that town recognized him, they sent word to the surrounding villages. People brought all those who were sick and begged Jesus to let them touch the hem of his robe. All who touched it were healed. Based on Matthew 14:34–36

? What Do You Wonder?

- Why do people get sick?
- Does Jesus work through some people to heal others?

Jesus Heals

How can faith lead to healing?

During his life, Jesus cared for people who were sick or in need of forgiveness. He healed people who had faith in him. Read this story about Jesus healing a man's daughter.

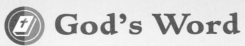 **God's Word**

Jesus Gives New Life

Jairus: Please let me through. I must talk to Jesus.

Woman: You look worried. Stand aside. Let this man through to see Jesus.

Jairus: Jesus, please. I beg you to come to my home. My only daughter is dying.

Jairus's servant: Jairus, I have sad news. Your daughter is dead.

Jesus: Jairus, don't be afraid. Have faith, and your daughter will be all right. [Jesus walks to Jairus's house.]

Jairus's wife: Jesus, thank you for coming to our home. Our daughter has died and we are very sad.

Jesus: She isn't dead. She is sleeping. Now everyone except her parents and my three friends must leave.

Crowd: He doesn't know what he's talking about. She really is dead!

Jesus: [touching the girl] Child, wake up! [The girl wakes up; her parents hug her.]

Jesus: Please don't tell anyone about what I did here today.

Jairus's wife: Thank you so much, Jesus! You have given us back our daughter. Based on Luke 8:40–42, 49–56

Share Your Faith

Think Reflect on the story of the healing of Jairus's daughter. Make a list of the type of scenery, the characters in the story, and the props you would need to act it out.

1. Scene: _____

2. Characters: _____

3. Props: _____

Share Act out the story with a small group.

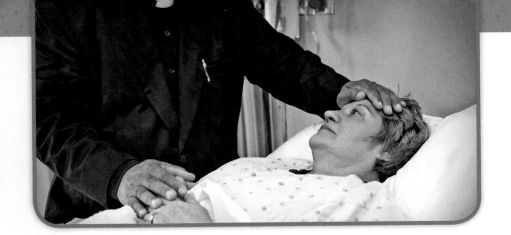

Signs of Healing

How do these Sacraments help us?

The **Sacraments of Healing** are Penance and Reconciliation and the Anointing of the Sick. These Sacraments help bring forgiveness and healing to those who are physically and spiritually sick.

During Penance, you confess your sins to a priest and are absolved (forgiven). In the Anointing of the Sick, the priest prays that God will send his healing love to the sick person. This Sacrament shows that all life is special and sacred.

Only a priest can preside at the Sacraments of Healing. Like all Sacraments, these Sacraments use words and actions to show God's love.

Catholic Faith Words

Sacraments of Healing Penance and Reconciliation and the Anointing of the Sick. In these Sacraments, God's forgiveness and healing are given to those suffering physical and spiritual sickness.

Sacraments of Healing

	Reconciliation	Anointing of the Sick
Actions	The priest extends his hand in blessing.	The priest uses the Oil of the Sick to anoint the head and hands of the person who is very sick or aged.
Words	"I absolve you from your sins in the name of the Father, and of the Son, and of the Holy Spirit."	"Through this holy anointing may the Lord in his love and mercy help you with the grace of the Holy Spirit. May the Lord who frees you from sin save you and raise you up."

Sin and Sickness

Sin and sickness are different in a very important way. Sickness may separate you from others, but you do not choose to be sick. When you sin, you make a choice to turn away from God and others; and you are responsible for that decision.

The effects of sin and sickness can be similar. Both can make you feel separated from God and from people you love. The Sacraments of Healing allow the community a chance to share your sorrows and joys. These Sacraments show God's mercy and our trust in his loving care. The Church prays for spiritual and physical healing from God.

Underline the effects of sin and sickness.

© Our Sunday Visitor

Connect Your Faith

Use Healing Words Sin and sickness often separate you in some way from those you love. Using the letters below, create words or phrases that tell how the Church helps you.

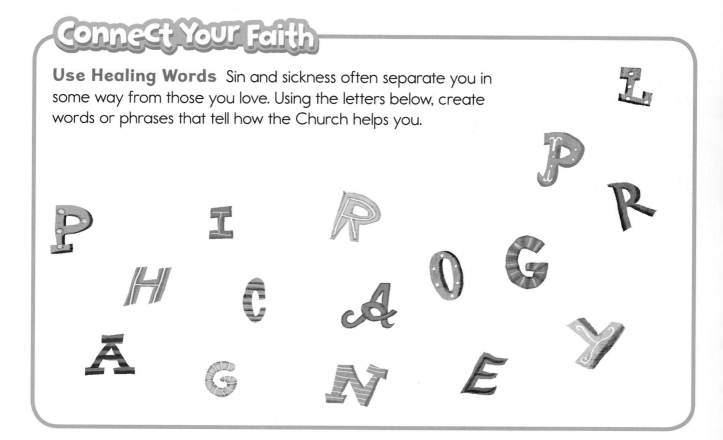

Our Catholic Life

How can you participate in the Sacraments of Healing?

Everyone has been hurt at one time or another. Healing from an injury can be fast or slow. The Sacraments of Healing are the Church's way to help those who need healing. Your parish celebrates the Sacraments of Healing often.

- Your parish might celebrate Reconciliation every week on Saturdays or before Mass.

- A priest may anoint someone who has been or may be sick for a long time.

- You can participate in Penance and Reconciliation whenever you need to. You may or may not need to receive the Sacrament of Anointing of the Sick in your lifetime.

- Both Sacraments of Healing give God's grace and help to strengthen you as a follower of Jesus.

Priests anoint those who are aged or seriously ill with the Oil of the Sick.

People of Faith

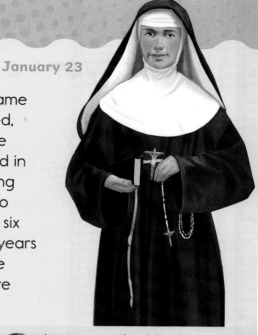

Saint Marianne Cope, 1838–1918

Saint Marianne Cope was born in Germany, but came to the United States as a baby. After her father died, she helped raise her brothers and sisters. When she was 24, she became a Franciscan sister. She worked in hospitals in New York. One day she learned that King Kalakaua of Hawaii was asking for sisters to come to the islands to work with lepers. Saint Marianne and six other sisters traveled to Honolulu. She spent many years caring for lepers on the island of Molokai. This is the same island where Saint Father Damien helped care for those dying of leprosy.

Discuss: What do you do when you are sick? How can Jesus make you feel better?

 Learn more about Saint Marianne Cope at **aliveinchrist.osv.com**

Live Your Faith

Write a Story of Healing Write a short story about a child who receives one of the Sacraments of Healing.

_____

_____

_____

_____

_____

_____

_____

_____

 **Let Us Pray**

Prayer for Healing

Gather and begin with the Sign of the Cross.

Leader: God wants us to ask for what we need in prayer. We pray now for those people we know who need God's healing.

Reader 1: Loving God, you take every family under your care.

Reader 2: You know our physical and spiritual needs.

All: Strengthen us with your grace so that we may grow in faith and love.

Reader 1: Loving God, you provide comfort for those who are sick.

Reader 2: You give them courage and peace.

All: Strengthen them with your grace so that they may know your love and care.

Reader 1: We ask this through our Lord Jesus Christ, your Son,

Reader 2: Who lives and reigns with you and the Holy Spirit.

All: One God, forever and ever. Amen.

Based on a prayer from the *Rite of the Anointing of the Sick*

 Sing "Heal Us, Lord"
Heal us, Lord.
We feel the power of your love.
Let your Spirit come unto us.

YOUR CHILD LEARNED >>>

This chapter describes the words and actions of the Sacraments of Healing: Penance and Reconciliation and the Anointing of the Sick.

God's Word

 Read **Matthew 14:34–36** and discuss any healing you may need.

Catholics Believe

• In the Sacraments of Healing, God's forgiveness and healing are given to those suffering physical and spiritual sickness.

• In Penance, a priest absolves sin. In the Anointing of the Sick, the priest anoints and prays for God to send his healing love.

To learn more, go to the *Catechism of the Catholic Church* #1420, 1421, 1424 at **usccb.org**.

People of Faith

This week, your child met Saint Marianne Cope, who worked to help sick people in New York and, later, lepers in Hawaii.

CHILDREN AT THIS AGE >>>

How They Understand the Sacraments of Healing

As mentioned in earlier chapters, the beginning awareness of community is characteristic of third-graders. Because of this, children this age can see the Sacraments of Healing as a way in which the Catholic community shows its care for those who are in need of physical and spiritual healing. This is also a good time to raise awareness of ways in which your child can personally show care to someone who is suffering through direct actions and through prayer.

CONSIDER THIS >>>

Have you ever prayed for someone to be healed?

We suffer when we see others in pain. The sense of helplessness and sorrow moves us to turn to God for help. "When the Sacrament of Anointing of the Sick is given the hoped-for effect is that, if it be God's will, the person be physically healed of illness. But even if there is no physical healing, the primary effect of the Sacrament is a spiritual healing by which the sick person receives the Holy Spirit's gift of peace and courage to deal with the difficulties that accompany serious illness or the frailty of old age" *(USCCA, p. 254).*

LET'S TALK >>>

• Talk about a time when someone you know has been anointed while they were sick.

• Ask your child to name some ways that the Sacraments of Healing can help people.

LET'S PRAY >>>

 Saint Marianne Cope, help us to be kind and loving to all who are sick. Amen.

 For a multimedia glossary of Catholic Faith Words, Sunday readings, seasonal and Saint resources, and chapter activities go to **aliveinchrist.osv.com**.

A **Work with Words** Complete each sentence with the correct word from the Word Bank.

1. During Penance and Reconciliation you confess your sins and are _____.

2. Illness, such as a cold or flu, is called _____ sickness.

3. Only a _____ can perform a Sacrament of Healing.

4. _____ is choosing to turn away from God.

5. Living with sin and not participating in Reconciliation can be called _____ sickness.

Word Bank

priest

forgiven

sin

physical

spiritual

B **Check Understanding** Write the letter T if the sentence is TRUE. Write the letter F if the sentence is FALSE.

6. Faith in Jesus' healing power was important in the story of Jairus's daughter. ☐

7. Penance is a Sacrament of Initiation. ☐

8. The Sacraments of Healing bring forgiveness and healing to those who are physically and spiritually sick. ☐

9. Oil is used for Penance and Reconciliation. ☐

10. The Sacraments show God's mercy and loving care. ☐

Go to **aliveinchrist.osv.com** for an interactive review.

Sacraments at the Service of Communion

 Let Us Pray

Leader: Dear God, we are your servants forever.

"The LORD is the redeemer of the souls of
   his servants;
and none are condemned who take
   refuge in him." **Psalm 34:23**

All: You want us to serve each other, Jesus. Let my heart
be like yours so that I serve out of love and not
because "I have to." Amen.

 God's Word

For you were called to be free. Do not use
this freedom so you can sin. Instead, serve
each other in love. For all the commandments
can be put together in one statement,
"You shall love your neighbor as
yourself." **Based on Galatians 5:13–14**

? **What Do You Wonder?**

- How can third-graders serve others in love?

- How will you know whether God is calling you to be married or to the priesthood or religious life?

Learning about Service

How do married people and ordained men serve others?

An anniversary is a time to remember a special day of love and commitment. Listen as Jeremy and Samantha learn about their parents' wedding day.

The Wedding Story

"Mom, you looked pretty," Samantha said.

"It's because I was so happy," said her mother.

"We said our **vows** and promised to love each other and to be faithful before God through good and bad times," Dad said.

"I know it's fun to share good times," said Samantha. "But bad times?"

"Well, Samantha," said Mom, "everyone has bad times, but mine would be worse if I didn't have your dad. We often ask God to help us through the bad times. And the good times are even better because I get to share them with someone I love."

Catholic Faith Words

vows solemn promises that are made to or before God

Sharing Wedding Memories

"Look, there's a picture of Father Hernandez, witnessing our wedding vows," said Mom. "He also met with us before we were married. He shared with us how important it is to understand that marriage is a Sacrament. That means that God gives us the grace to love each other and help each other grow in his image. Our **priest** and **deacon** do a lot of work that we don't always see."

"What kind of work?" asked Jeremy.

"They teach people about the faith and guide them in making good decisions. They visit people who are sick and serve the parish in many other ways. Priests celebrate Mass and other Sacraments. Deacons baptize and witness marriages. Priests and deacons do important work," said Dad.

"Just like married people," said Samantha.

"Yes, just like married people. God helps all of us do his work," said Mom.

Catholic Faith Words

priest an ordained man who helps his bishop by leading a parish, preaching the Gospel, and celebrating the Eucharist and other Sacraments

deacon an ordained man who serves the Church by assisting in the Eucharist, baptizing, witnessing marriages, and doing works of charity

Share Your Faith

Think What is love? Think about the different ways that people show love to one another.

Share with a partner about the different meanings of love and how you can show love for others.

Serving God's People

How do the Sacraments at the Service of Communion continue Jesus' work?

The priest and the parents in the story had something in common. They had each celebrated one of the **Sacraments at the Service of Communion**. The two Sacraments are Holy Orders and Matrimony.

Holy Orders is the Sacrament in which baptized men become deacons, priests, or bishops. When a man receives Holy Orders, he is ordained. He shares Jesus' ministry in a special way. Saint Paul wrote about the work of the Church's early ministers.

Circle the two Sacraments at the Service of Communion.

Catholic Faith Words

Sacraments at the Service of Communion the two sacraments that celebrate people's commitment to serve God and the community: Holy Orders and Matrimony

God's Word

The place of the preachers is not to establish themselves as leaders among men; instead, think of us as servants of Christ and trustworthy stewards of the mysteries of God. Based on 1 Corinthians 3:21–4:2

➡ **What are some ways deacons, priests, and bishops serve the Church?**

Sacraments of Service

	Holy Orders	Matrimony
Action	A bishop lays his hands on the man to be ordained and prays to the Holy Spirit.	In front of a priest or deacon and other witnesses, a baptized woman and man promise to love each other and to be faithful.
Effects	The ordained man receives the authority to minister, to teach, and to lead and serve the Church and their community through sacramental ministries and works of charity.	The couple receives the grace to love each other as Christ loves his Church, to remain faithful, and to welcome and raise children.

Serving One Another

Married people share Jesus' ministry, too. The Sacrament of Matrimony joins a baptized man and a baptized woman in Christian marriage. They serve God by loving and serving each other and any children God gives them.

Sometimes husbands and wives must both work at jobs so that their families will have food and shelter. Other times, one of them may stay home with their children while the other goes to work.

Sometimes a couple has to live apart from each other. However, they must still do their best to serve their families. The Church cares for and supports all families.

Through the Sacraments of Baptism and Confirmation, all Church members are called to use their gifts to serve God's People. Any way you answer that call, you serve God and your community.

Connect Your Faith

Learn About Sacraments at the Service of Communion In this space, write two questions that you would like to ask your pastor and a married person about how they serve others.

_____

_____

Our Catholic Life

How can you serve the family of God?

Being part of a family brings many responsibilities. Being part of God's family, the Church, brings responsibilities, too. Many people serve through their vocation to marriage or through Holy Orders.

When you serve others, you do not think about how the service will help you. You serve others because God calls you to share your time and talents with others.

You can serve others through small acts of kindness. You can assist a neighbor by carrying groceries. You can help your parents care for your brothers or sisters or a pet. There are many ways to serve God and others.

© Our Sunday Visitor

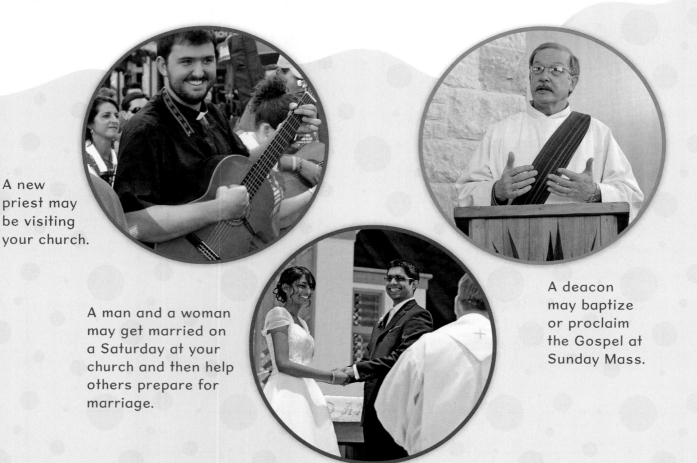

A new priest may be visiting your church.

A man and a woman may get married on a Saturday at your church and then help others prepare for marriage.

A deacon may baptize or proclaim the Gospel at Sunday Mass.

People of Faith

Saint Jean-Baptiste de la Salle, 1651–1719

Saint Jean-Baptiste de la Salle knew he wanted to be a priest when he was eleven years old. He came from a wealthy French family. He used his money to build schools for poor children. He founded a group of men called the Christian Brothers, who were teachers. He also founded a college to train teachers. He said that when he became a priest, he didn't know he would be a teacher, too. He knew he had a vocation to be a priest, but God also gave him a vocation to teach. Even today, Christian Brothers teach in schools all around the world.

April 7

Discuss: How have you served the poor?

 Learn more about Saint Jean-Baptiste de la Salle at **aliveinchrist.osv.com**

Live Your Faith

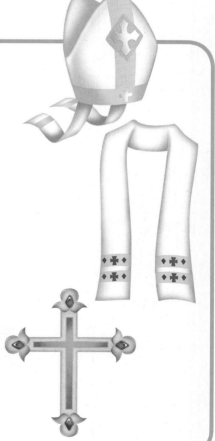

Write a Thank You Letter Bishops, priests, and deacons do many things for Church members. Draft a thank-you letter to one of these leaders. Then write your final letter on nice paper and send it to the person.

_____

_____

_____

_____

_____

_____

_____

Let Us Pray

Prayer of Thanks

Gather and begin with the Sign of the Cross.

Leader: Generous God, we thank you for the gifts of service of bishops, priests, deacons, and married people.

Reader 1: For priests who lead us to you,

All: We thank you, God.

Reader 2: For deacons who help us find you,

All: We thank you, God.

Reader 3: For bishops who guide your people,

All: We thank you, God.

Reader 4: For married people who lead each other to you,

All: We thank you, God.

Reader 5: For parents who show us how to love you,

All: We thank you, God.

 Sing "All That God Wants You to Be"
You can become all that
God wants you to be!

Here am I, O Lord! I come
to do your will.
Help me become all that
you want me to be!
© 2006, Carey Landry. Published by OCP.
All rights reserved.

FAMILY+FAITH
LIVING AND LEARNING TOGETHER

YOUR CHILD LEARNED >>>

This chapter explores serving God and the community through the Sacraments at the Service of Communion: Holy Orders and Matrimony.

God's Word

Read **Galatians 5:13–14** to learn more about how we should serve one another.

Catholics Believe

- Holy Orders is the Sacrament in which baptized men are ordained as deacons, priests, or bishops to lead and serve the Church.

- Matrimony joins a baptized man and a baptized woman in Christian marriage to serve God by loving and serving each other and any children they may have.

To learn more, go to the *Catechism of the Catholic Church* #1534, 1535 at **usccb.org**.

People of Faith

This week, your child met Saint Jean-Baptiste de la Salle, a priest, teacher, and the founder of the Christian Brothers, whose mission is to educate youth.

CHILDREN AT THIS AGE >>>

How They Understand the Sacraments at the Service of Communion Your child's emerging awareness of others makes this an ideal time to consider how God might call him or her to serve others in the Church and in society. Particular consideration should be given to Matrimony, Holy Orders, or religious life. While your child will ultimately have many years to discern a vocation, an early awareness of a life of service can help keep your child oriented in a direction that is compatible with God's plan for his or her life.

CONSIDER THIS >>>

In how many ways do you see yourself as a servant?

If you are a parent you may see your whole life through the eyes of service! The choice is in being begrudging angry servants, or eager servants, knowing that our service is an act of love. "God's people share in Christ's kingly mission, which is to lead others through loving service to them. Jesus came not 'to be served but to serve and to give his life as a ransom for many' (Mt 20:28). We are called in imitation of the Lord Jesus, to be people who offer ourselves willingly in service to others" (*USCCA, p. 118*).

LET'S TALK >>>

- Ask your child to name some ways that the people in your family serve God and others.

- Share some good memories of weddings and family life that you have seen or experienced.

LET'S PRAY >>>

 Saint Jean-Baptiste, help us know what God is calling us to do. May we listen to that call and willingly follow it. Amen.

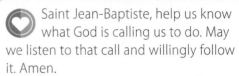 For a multimedia glossary of Catholic Faith Words, Sunday readings, seasonal and Saint resources, and chapter activities go to **aliveinchrist.osv.com**.

Chapter 18 Review

A **Work with Words** Complete each sentence with the letter of the correct word or words from the Word Bank.

Word Bank

a. vows

b. Holy Orders

c. Service

d. ordained

e. deacon

1. A baptized man is ☐ during the Sacrament of Holy Orders.

2. The ☐ made during the Sacrament of Matrimony last a lifetime.

3. Only baptized men are called to receive ☐ .

4. Holy Orders celebrates a man's commitment to Jesus' ministry as a ☐ , priest, or bishop.

5. The two Sacraments at the ☐ of Communion celebrate people's commitment to serve God and the community.

B **Check Understanding** Match each description in Column A with the correct term in Column B.

Column A

6. What a man is called after the Sacrament of Matrimony

7. Ordains a baptized man

8. The Sacrament that unites a man and woman in love and faithfulness

9. Ordained man who leads a parish

10. Solemn promises made before God

Column B

Holy Orders

priest

husband

Matrimony

vows

Go to **aliveinchrist.osv.com** for an interactive review.

A **Work with Words** Write the correct answer to complete each sentence.

1. _____ are solemn promises that are made to or before God.

2. Sacraments at the _____ of Communion celebrate people's commitment to serve God and the community.

3. _____ are signs that come from Jesus and give grace.

4. Sacraments of _____ celebrate membership into the Catholic Church.

5. Sacred _____ is perfumed oil used for anointing in the Sacraments of Baptism, Confirmation, and Holy Orders.

Complete the chart below with the names of the Sacraments.

Sacraments	
Initiation	**Healing**
6. _____	9. _____
7. _____	_____
8. _____	10. _____

B **Check Understanding** Match each description in Column A with the correct Sacrament in Column B.

Column A	Column B
11. Received by people who are very sick	Penance and Reconciliation
12. Removes Original Sin, forgives personal sin, and gives new life in Christ	Baptism
13. Unites a person more fully with Christ	Eucharist
14. Celebrates the gift of the Body and Blood of Christ in Holy Communion	Confirmation
15. Absolves you of your sins	Anointing of the Sick

Write the letter T if the sentence is TRUE. Write the letter F if the sentence is FALSE.

16. ☐ In the Sacrament of the Eucharist we honor Christ's Real Presence in Holy Communion.

17. ☐ Confirmation strengthens our bond with the Church.

18. ☐ Jesus did not want to help those who were sick or in need.

19. ☐ Only a deacon can preside at the Sacraments of Healing.

20. ☐ When a man receives Holy Orders, he is ordained.

© Our Sunday Visitor

C **Make Connections** Write responses to each question or statement on the lines below.

21. Name a person who has received the Sacrament of Holy Orders, and tell one way in which he serves others.

_____

_____

22. What did you learn from the story of Jairus and his daughter?

_____

_____

23. Why is celebrating the Eucharist important?

_____

_____

24. How do married couples serve God and others?

_____

_____

_____

25. How can an unmarried person serve God?

_____

_____

_____

Kingdom of God

Our Catholic Tradition

- The Church is a sign of God's covenant. (CCC, 762)

- We share in the Church's mission to spread the Good News. (CCC, 852)

- We are all signs of God's Kingdom. (CCC, 567)

- If we die in God's friendship, we will live with him forever. (CCC, 1023)

- At the end of the world, Christ will judge all people by how they lived their lives. (CCC, 681)

How does the covenant that God made with Abraham continue in Jesus and throughout the Church?

The Church Through Time

Let Us Pray

Leader: Faithful God, help us to follow your path of love.

"All the paths of the LORD are mercy and truth toward those who honor his covenant and decrees." **Psalm 25:10**

All: O God, you promised to always be with us. Give us the strength to live our promise to put you first in our lives. Amen.

God's Word

After Jesus went to Heaven, his followers asked the Apostles to teach them all that Jesus had said. They lived together sharing all their things. They gathered to pray and to bless, break, and share the bread. **Based on Acts 2:42**

❓ What Do You Wonder?

• Is God always with you?

• How are you a part of God's plan to share the news of his Son, Jesus?

God's Covenant

How does God care for his People?

The beginnings of the Church's history go back to ancient times. Here is the story of the time when God first called his People.

Catholic Faith Words

covenant a sacred promise or agreement between God and humans

proclaim to tell about Jesus in words and actions

Underline God's promises to Abraham.

 **God's Word**

I Will Be Your God

Sarai and Abram were sad. They had no children. One night Abram went outside and he heard God call to him. God said, "Abram, I want to make a promise to you, a covenant. I will be your God and you will become the father of many people."

Abram said to God, "You know that Sarai and I trust you, but we are old and we have no children."

God said, "I want to begin a covenant with you. You will now be called Abraham. You will become the father of many nations. Your wife's name will now be Sarah. I will bless her and give you a son."

> God told Abraham to look up at the stars. He then said, "Your family will outnumber the stars. They will be my People, and I will be their God. All nations will be blessed through you. This is my covenant, my promise to you." Based on Genesis 17:1–19

Fulfilled in Jesus

God kept his promise. Abraham and Sarah had a son. Their family grew and they were God's Chosen People, the people of Israel. God was faithful to the **covenant**, the sacred promise, he had made with Abraham.

When Jesus, God's own Son, was born, God the Father extended the covenant to all people. Through Jesus' Death, Resurrection, and Ascension, God's promise was fulfilled. All people were saved from the power of sin and everlasting death through Jesus.

Followers of Jesus tell others about him in their words and actions. They **proclaim** the Good News of God's Kingdom and are a sign of his covenant.

Share Your Faith

Think Write a promise you will make to God.

_____

_____

_____

Share Take turns sharing your thoughts with a partner.

259

The Early Church

How did the Church grow?

Jesus and his first followers were Jewish. After Jesus returned to the Father, some of his followers continued to attend Jewish services on the Sabbath. They also gathered to celebrate the Eucharist in secret places like their homes or hidden catacombs.

The followers of Christ became known as Christians. They saw themselves as a new people, as the Church. Christians spread the Good News to other lands.

The early years of the Church were times of persecution, when many Christians were imprisoned or put to death. Even in difficult times, Jesus' followers were loyal to their promises to God. They were **faithful** to him and to the covenant.

➤ **Why is it important to learn about the early Christians?**

© Our Sunday Visitor

Catholic Faith Words

faithful to be constant and loyal to your promises and commitments to God and others, just as he is faithful to you

The ruins at Dura Europos in Syria, one of the earliest known house churches where Christians gathered.

The Church Grows

Christians kept the Church alive and growing. When invaders from the North attacked Rome, Christians in Ireland and Scotland kept the Gospel alive in monasteries. Many Saints, including Patrick, Brigid, Kevin, and Columba, helped to carry on the Church's mission.

Into the Present

Many Saints you have read about this year in People of Faith have bravely carried the Word of God to distant lands. The Catholic faith has spread throughout Africa, Asia, Europe, and the Americas.

The Church's history is still being written today. You and all people who follow Jesus are an important part of the story of faith as well.

Mass of the Chrism at Saint Mary's Church in Secunderabad, India.

Connect Your Faith

Reflect How do people know that you are a Catholic?

People know that I am a follower of Jesus because:

_____

My parish family shows that it follows Jesus by:

_____

When I think of Catholics, I think of:

_____

Our Catholic Life

What can you learn from the Church's past?

It can be fun to find out how people lived long ago. Studying the past can help you understand people's ideas and actions. You can learn how people solved problems. Their ideas can help you see how to solve problems today.

Dig into the Past

Think of a time in Church history that you would like to learn more about, or think of a Saint or another person who did special work for the Church.

Research a topic about Church history. Place a check mark next to it and write one reason you chose it.

Church History Research Topics

- [ ] **One of the Apostles**

- [ ] **Missions to Africa and Asia**

- [ ] **Saint Patrick, Saint Brigid, Saint Kevin, or Saint Columba**

- [ ] **Blessed Junipero Serra**

- [ ] **Padre Eusebio Kino**

_____

_____

_____

People of Faith

Saint Clement of Rome, died c. A.D. 100 November 23

Saint Clement was the bishop of Rome. He was one of the first Popes after Saint Peter. In fact, he learned about Jesus from Saint Peter himself. One of the things we know about Saint Clement is that he wrote a special letter. It was sent to Christians in a place called Corinth. It is one of the oldest letters we have from a Pope. In it, he talks about the Eucharist. Sometimes you will hear Saint Clement's name read in a list of Saints during Mass.

Discuss: How does the Pope communicate to people today?

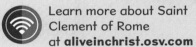 Learn more about Saint Clement of Rome at **aliveinchrist.osv.com**

Live Your Faith

Record Your Findings Record information you've learned about the topic you chose to research.

My topic:

_____

Why this topic interests me:

_____

What I learned:

_____

_____

Why this topic is important to Church history:

_____

_____

 **Let Us Pray**

Prayer of Faith

Gather and begin with the Sign of the Cross.

Leader: God our Father, we remember today our ancestors who have walked in faith with you.

Reader 1: Faith is getting what we have hoped for. It is our hope of what we have not seen.

Reader 2: By faith, we believe that God created the world.

Reader 3: By faith, Noah built an ark when he could see no water.

Reader 1: By faith, Abraham obeyed when God sent him to a faraway place.

Reader 2: By faith, Moses led God's People across the Red Sea as if it were dry land.

Reader 3: Yet God had something even better for his People.
Based on Hebrews 11

All: Thanks be to God.

 Sing "Get on the Boat"
Get on the boat! Get on the boat!
Get on! Noah, tell your friends.
Get on the boat! Get on the boat
before the rain begins.
© 1999, Mark Friedman and Janet Vogt.
Published by OCP. All rights reserved.

FAMILY+FAITH
LIVING AND LEARNING TOGETHER

YOUR CHILD LEARNED >>>

This chapter examines the covenant between Abraham and God and recalls that, through Jesus, the Church continues to be a sign of God's everlasting covenant.

God's Word

 Read **Acts 2:42** and learn how the early Christians lived and worshipped together.

Catholics Believe

• God kept his promise to be forever faithful when he sent his Son, Jesus.

• Throughout her history, the Church strives to be faithful to God's covenant and proclaim the Good News.

To learn more, go to the *Catechism of the Catholic Church* #781, 1612 at **usccb.org**.

People of Faith

This week, your child met Saint Clement, one of the first Popes after Saint Peter.

CHILDREN AT THIS AGE >>>

How They Understand the Historical Church Learning about their faith ancestors and the great things they have done can be exciting for third-graders, who enjoy feeling a part of something larger than themselves. It's helpful if children this age can place themselves within the context of the story, for example in the way that they are emulating a particular Saint in their own talents, actions, or goals for the future.

CONSIDER THIS >>>

How important is it to keep your promises to others?

Being able to trust someone to keep their promise of faithfulness or dependability is the foundation of a relationship. A sacred promise is called a covenant. "The covenant between God and humanity was first established with Noah after the great Flood,... God entered into a covenant later with Abraham and then with the people of Israel at the time of their exodus from slavery in Egypt under the leadership of Moses. He affirmed that they will always be his people" (*USCCA, p. 14*).

LET'S TALK >>>

• Ask your child to describe the covenant between God and the people of Israel.

• Talk about a Saint or someone you've learned about who did special work for the Church.

LET'S PRAY >>>

 Saint Clement, pray for us that we may stand up for our faith. Help us remember all the Christians who lived before us and taught us about the faith. Amen.

For a multimedia glossary of Catholic Faith Words, Sunday readings, seasonal and Saint resources, and chapter activities go to **aliveinchrist.osv.com**.

Chapter 19 Review

A **Work with Words** Fill in the circle beside the correct answer.

1. God made a covenant with _____.

   ○ Isaac   ○ Abraham

2. A covenant is a sacred _____ between God and humans.

   ○ agreement   ○ sacrifice

3. Jesus and his first followers were _____.

   ○ Jewish   ○ Christian

4. Followers of Christ became known as _____.

   ○ Jews   ○ Christians

5. Jesus _____ the covenant between God and his People.

   ○ destroyed   ○ fulfilled

B **Check Understanding** Write the letter T if the sentence is TRUE. Write the letter F if the sentence is False.

6. ☐ There is no way to learn more about Church history or people from the past who have done special work for the Church.

7. ☐ Early Jewish Christians met to pray at Jewish services and in homes.

8. ☐ Early Christians shared their faith and were sometimes persecuted for doing so.

9. ☐ The Church's history is still being written today.

10. ☐ The Church never spread out of Israel.

Go to **aliveinchrist.osv.com** for an interactive review.

The Work of the Church

 **Let Us Pray**

Leader: God our Father, help us build your Church.

"The stone the builders rejected
has become the cornerstone." Psalm 118:22

All: Jesus, through Baptism we have become members of your Body, the Church. Help us to always remember that you are the center of our lives. Amen.

 **God's Word**

Be happy! Change your bad habits, encourage each other, be agreeable with each other, live in peace. The God of love and peace is always with you.

Based on 2 Corinthians 13:11

? **What Do You Wonder?**

- What does Saint Paul mean by live in peace?

- What would make people stop fighting so that we could have peace in the world?

267

Doing Jesus' Work

What is the Church called to do?

Jesus sent his disciples on a mission to spread the Good News and gave them special instructions.

 God's Word

The Commissioning of the Twelve

Jesus sent his disciples on a mission to spread the Good News. These are the instructions he gave them.

Travel to visit the people of Israel. Tell them that the Kingdom of God is at hand. Cure people who are sick. Don't take supplies or extra clothes or sandals. Whenever you come to a town, find a good person's home, and stay there as long as you are in the town. When you go into a house, bless it. If people do not accept you or listen to you, leave the house or town and have nothing to do with it. **Based on Matthew 10:5–14**

The Church helps to continue Jesus' work on Earth. Our work is to worship God, to help others know and worship God the Father, Son, and Holy Spirit, and to live holy lives. We are called to help and protect all life, especially the lives of those who are most vulnerable and those who are poor. We are called to work for peace and justice.

Called to Work

Each of us has talents, gifts, and interests that God has given us. They can be a call from God to do a particular kind of work for his Church.

⭐ Fill in the blanks with ways you can share your time, talent, and treasure.

Give Your Time, Talent, and Treasure

What are some of the talents and gifts God has given you?

_____

_____

What are some of the things that interest you most?

_____

_____

How can you use your talents and interests to help in the work of the Church?

_____

_____

Share Your Faith

Think What instructions would you give fellow disciples on how to follow Christ and be members of the Catholic Church?

Share Share your ideas with the other groups.

The Church in the World

How does the Church do Jesus' work in the world today?

You know that there are many problems in the world. Some of the problems are so big that you may think someone your age can't help solve them or make a difference. Think about the Twelve who set out with Jesus' Good News.

Every time you work as the disciples did to help others know God you are working for God's Kingdom. Every time you encourage someone to turn to God in prayer, feed a person who is hungry, stop a fight, or give someone hope, you are sharing the Good News of Jesus.

The Catholic faith is about the past, future, and present. Right here, right now, the Holy Spirit is with us, and we are the Church.

Place a check mark next to the things you can do right now to be part of the work of the Church.

Working for God's Kingdom

- [ ] helping people worship God
- [ ] teaching people about God
- [ ] sending missionaries to other places to share the Gospel
- [ ] standing up for people's rights for life, water, work, and freedom
- [ ] helping those who are poor or in need

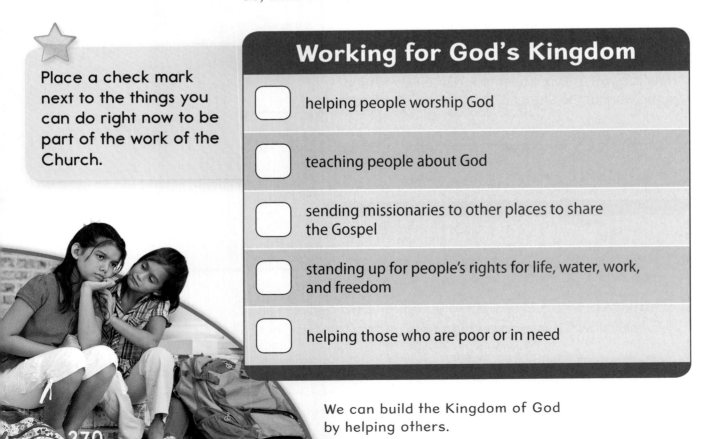

We can build the Kingdom of God by helping others.

Sharing a Mission

The mission of the Church is to share the Good News, make the world holy, and serve God and one another. The Church is a sign of God's Kingdom. She helps people share in the love of the Holy Trinity. Your words and actions show God's **justice**, love, and **peace**. You are asked to do this at your Baptism.

As a member of the Church, you join in her work. The Spirit strengthens you to tell others about Jesus. You can help the Church worship God in the Mass. You can work for everyone's basic rights, such as food, clothing, shelter, and life and dignity. You can care for people who are poor, ill, or lonely.

Why Help with the Church's Work?

When you help with the Church's mission, you follow the example of Jesus. You do this because you love God and put him first. You also do this because all people are your sisters and brothers. God calls all people to be united in his family and to share what they have.

Catholic Faith Words

justice giving God what is due to him, and giving each person what he or she is due because that person is a child of God

peace a state of calm when things are in their proper order and people settle problems with kindness and justice

Connect Your Faith

Send a Message Design a T-shirt that helps spread the message about the Church's mission.

Our Catholic Life

How do you give witness?

Through Baptism, all Catholics are called to live their faith every day. This is known as giving witness. Sometimes giving witness can be done without saying anything.

Living your faith means acting according to your beliefs, with the Holy Spirit's help, to bring the Good News of God's Kingdom to the world. You can give witness to your faith throughout your community.

Write two more ways that you can give witness in your community.

Get Involved

- Volunteer with other members of your church to clean up a local park.
- Do small jobs or chores for a neighbor who is sick or elderly.
- Show respect for others by using good manners.

- _____
- _____
_____
- _____
_____

People of Faith

Saint Peter Claver, 1581–1654

September 9

Saint Peter Claver was from Spain. He moved to Columbia and became a Jesuit priest. When slave ships came from Africa, Saint Peter would meet them at the docks to give the slaves food and medicine. He would tell the slaves how much God loved them and talk to them about Jesus. He wanted to stop all slavery but until that happened, he made sure slaves were given food and clothes and treated kindly. He also helped sick people in the hospital, prisoners in jail, and sailors.

Discuss: To whom can you bring God's message of love?

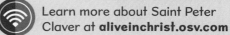 Learn more about Saint Peter Claver at **aliveinchrist.osv.com**

Live Your Faith

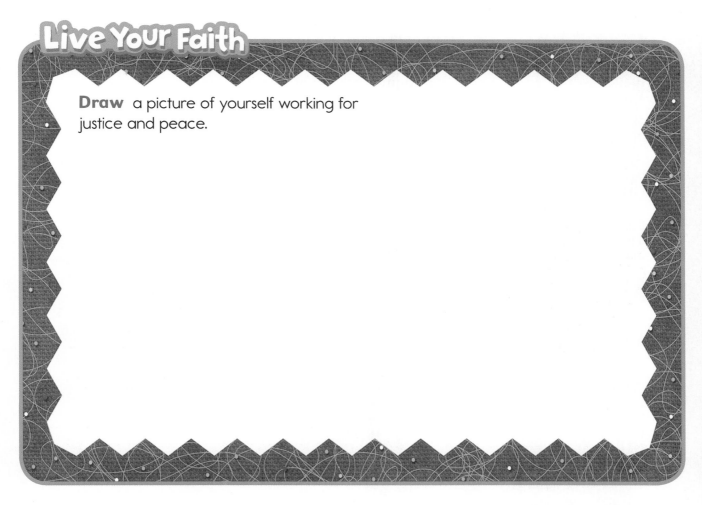

Draw a picture of yourself working for justice and peace.

 **Let Us Pray**

Prayer for Peace

Gather and begin with the Sign of the Cross.

All: Pray together.
Lord, make me an instrument of your peace;
where there is hatred, let me sow love;
where there is injury, pardon;
where there is doubt, faith;
where there is despair, hope;
where there is darkness, light;
and where there is sadness, joy.

Grant that I may not so much seek
to be consoled as to console,
to be understood as to understand,
to be loved as to love;
for it is in giving that we receive,
it is in pardoning that we are pardoned,
and it is in dying that we are born to eternal life. Amen.
Prayer of Saint Francis

 Sing "Peace Is Flowing Like a River"
Peace is flowing like a river,
flowing out of you and me.
Flowing out into the desert,
setting all the captives free.

His love is flowing…
Alleluia, Alleluia…

Traditional, adapted by Carey Landry.
Text and music adaptation
© 1975, 1979, OCP.
All rights reserved.

FAMILY+FAITH
LIVING AND LEARNING TOGETHER

YOUR CHILD LEARNED >>>

This chapter recalls that all members of the Church share in her mission to work for peace and justice and Jesus' instruction to his disciples to share the Good News.

God's Word

 Read **2 Corinthians 13:11** and see ways that we can help and encourage one another.

Catholics Believe

• We can use our time, talent, and treasure to worship God, help others know about him, and respect and help others.

• The Church is a sign of the Kingdom of God.

To learn more, go to the *Catechism of the Catholic Church* #2044–2046 at **usccb.org**.

People of Faith

This week, your child met Saint Peter Claver who helped African slaves when they arrived in the Americas.

CHILDREN AT THIS AGE >>>

How They Understand the Work of the Church Today In our increasingly secular society, children may view the Church as quite separate from everyday life. It is important that we talk about our identity as members of the Catholic community and how this identity is one we carry with us into all places and situations. This calls us to responsibility. We are Jesus' voice, hands, and feet in the world.

CONSIDER THIS >>>

When have you experienced the peace that Jesus alone can give?

People describe peace in many ways including a lack of conflict or everyone just doing what they want. Jesus reminds us that the peace he alone can give comes from the hard work of dying to our ego. "Jesus' life, teaching, death, and Resurrection show us the meaning of love and justice in a broken world. Sacred Scripture and traditional ethical principles define what it means to make peace" *(Living with Faith and Hope after September 11, 2001,* quoted in *USCCA, p. 332).*

LET'S TALK >>>

• Ask your child what he or she can do right now to follow Jesus' example.

• Discuss some ways your family can share their time, talent, and treasure.

LET'S PRAY >>>

 Dear God, lead us to be like Saint Peter Claver and help those who are hungry or sick. Amen.

 For a multimedia glossary of Catholic Faith Words, Sunday readings, seasonal and Saint resources, and chapter activities go to **aliveinchrist.osv.com**.

Chapter 20 Review

A **Work with Words** Find the five basic rights of all humans listed in the Word Bank in the word search below.

Word Bank

food

shelter

clothing

diginity

life

1–5.

D	F	Y	L	W	I	B	G
M	I	I	K	R	G	N	I
X	F	G	A	A	I	F	A
E	E	S	N	H	T	O	U
G	M	R	T	I	D	O	X
T	J	O	X	P	T	D	A
W	L	A	M	O	Q	Y	A
C	S	H	E	L	T	E	R

B **Check Understanding** Match each description in Column A with the correct term in Column B.

Column A

6. Giving God and others what's due to them

7. Settling problems with kindness; a state of calm

8. Share the Good News

9. Sign of God's Kingdom

10. Living your faith

Column B

the Church

giving witness

justice

peace

our mission

Go to **aliveinchrist.osv.com** for an interactive review.

Everlasting Life

 Let Us Pray

Leader: Loving Father, we praise your name forever.

"Your reign is a reign for all ages,
your dominion for all generations." Psalm 145:13

All: By his Death and Resurrection, Jesus gave us eternal life. Loving Father, help us to live in this world in a way that reflects your goodness. Amen.

God's Word

And this is our belief. "God gave us eternal life, and this life is in his Son. Whoever knows Jesus has life."
Based on 1 John 5:11–12

? What Do You Wonder?

- What will Heaven be like?
- How would it feel to be separated from God's love forever?

Cycles of Life

What happens after death?

The cycle of life begins with birth and ends in death. Read this story about the cycle of life and dealing with loss.

The Little Daisy

Early one spring, a little bud named Daisy grew from a seed. She became friends with another bud named Sunflower.

Daisy grew into a small white flower with a little yellow head. Sunflower grew very tall with yellow petals and a large brown head. They both loved the fresh morning dew and the warm summer sun.

One day the wind got very cold. Daisy noticed that ice had formed on her leaves.

"What is happening?" she asked.

Sunflower said, "At the end of summer, it is time for us to die. When you die, your seeds will fall back into the ground and then new flowers will bloom from your seeds!"

"I feel much better now," said Daisy. She laid her head down and said, "I've had a beautiful life."

New Life

When Jesus came to Earth, he told people that if they believed in him, they would have everlasting life. His own Resurrection is the proof that his promise is true. His followers saw him alive after he had died. Later, John, who was one of Jesus' followers, had a vision from God of what would come at the end of time. This is what John said about his vision.

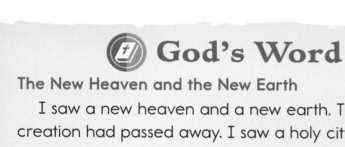 **God's Word**

The New Heaven and the New Earth

I saw a new heaven and a new earth. The old creation had passed away. I saw a holy city coming out of the sky. It was like a new Jerusalem. I heard God's voice saying that there would be no more tears or sadness, no more suffering or death.

Based on Revelation 21:1–4

 **Share Your Faith**

Think Unscramble the words to find John's vision of what the new Heaven and Earth will look like.

A LHYO YICT MGOINC UTO FO HTE YKS

☐ ☐ ☐ ☐ ☐ ☐ ☐ ☐ ☐ ☐ ☐ ☐ ☐ ☐

☐ ☐ ☐ ☐ ☐ ☐ ☐ ☐ ☐ ☐ ☐ ☐

Share your answer with a partner.

Our Future

What does the Church teach about life after death?

We look forward to a reunion with God. The Church looks beyond death to the coming of God's Kingdom in its fullness.

When we die we will be judged on our faith and works. This is called the Particular Judgment. God decides where each person will spend eternity: **Heaven**, **Hell**, or **Purgatory**. At the end of time, all people will be judged, as Jesus said. Those who have loved God and die in his friendship will ultimately live with him forever in Heaven.

As you look forward to good times on Earth, you can also look forward to Christ's Second Coming and the **Last Judgment**, when God will triumph over evil. Catholics live in hope that God's grace and our loving actions will lead to everlasting life with God in Heaven. Our trust in God gives us hope that we will be reunited with our loved ones.

Catholic Faith Words

Heaven the full joy of living with God forever

Hell being separated from God forever because of a choice to turn away from him and not seek forgiveness

Purgatory a state of final cleansing after death and before entering into Heaven

Last Judgment God's final triumph over evil that will occur at the end of time, when Christ returns and judges all the living and the dead

© Our Sunday Visitor

The Beginning and the End

The Bible begins and ends with stories of creation. In the Book of Genesis, the first book of the Bible, you read how God created all things out of love. The last book, the Book of Revelation, ends with John's vision of a new creation. This is God's everlasting Kingdom. The world and the Church will then be perfect. All faithful people will be raised to new life.

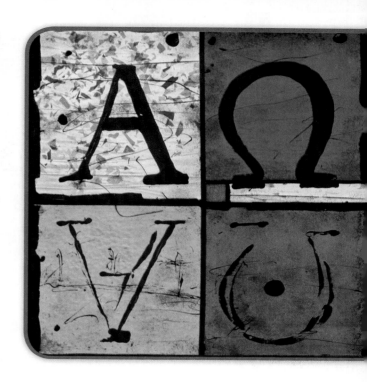

The Son of God, the Word of God, was present at the creation, and he will be present at the end of time. In John's vision, Jesus Christ says,

"I am the Alpha and the Omega, the first and the last, the beginning and the end." Revelation 22:13

Connect Your Faith

Share a Message Write a message to share with those who do not know God's love.

_____

_____

_____

_____

Our Catholic Life

How do you give comfort to others?

Even though there is life after death, people are usually sad when someone dies. The friends and family members of the person who has died are sad because they cannot see and talk with the person anymore. They know that it could be a long time before they meet their loved one in Heaven.

The Church asks you to find ways to comfort people who are sad because of a death.

Write one more way you can comfort someone.

Ways to Comfort

- Find ways to make their lives easier. Take them food, or help with chores around their homes.

- Visit the funeral home with your family, or go to the funeral.

- Talk about the person who died, telling why that person was special.

- Say that you are sorry about the death.

- _____

_____

People of Faith

Saint Joseph, first century

March 19

Saint Joseph was Mary's husband and the foster father of Jesus on Earth. When Jesus was a baby, Joseph took Jesus and Mary to Egypt to protect them from King Herod who wanted to kill Jesus. When Jesus was lost in the Temple at age 12, Joseph helped Mary look for Jesus. He was a carpenter and taught Jesus how to build things. We don't know how he died, but we believe that Mary and Jesus were with him. Today, we pray to Saint Joseph for a happy and peaceful death.

Discuss: Who do you know in your family who has died?

 Learn more about Saint Joseph at **aliveinchrist.osv.com**

Live Your Faith

Make a Card Use this space to design a sympathy card for someone who has recently lost a loved one. Decorate it with flowers or trees to represent new life. Include drawings, verses of Scripture, or a prayer.

 Let Us Pray

Prayer for the Kingdom

Gather and begin with the Sign of the Cross.

Leader: We gather and share a prayer for the coming of the Kingdom.

Reader 1: God, we have learned so much about you this year.

Reader 2: We have taught one another about your love.

Reader 3: Help us learn even more about you in school, at home, and at play.

Reader 1: Help us grow to be more caring people, who will show your love to all who know us.

Reader 2: When our earthly lives end, judge us by our loving deeds.

Reader 3: We hope to join your Saints and rejoice in your presence forever.

All: Come, Lord Jesus! Amen.

▶ Sing "Seek Ye First"

FAMILY+FAITH
LIVING AND LEARNING TOGETHER

YOUR CHILD LEARNED >>>

This chapter identifies the Last Judgment as God's final triumph over evil, when Christ will come again and bring the Kingdom of God to its fullness.

God's Word

 Read **1 John 5:11–12** to learn about the promise of eternal life that God shared with John.

Catholics Believe

- People who die in God's friendship will live forever in his presence.
- At the end of the world, Christ will judge all people on the way they lived their lives.

To learn more, go to the *Catechism of the Catholic Church* #1023–1029, 1039 at **usccb.org**.

People of Faith

This week, your child met Saint Joseph, the husband of Mary, and patron of happy and peaceful death.

CHILDREN AT THIS AGE >>>

How They Understand Life after Death One of the most common and intense fears of children in third grade (although it is usually unspoken) is that someone close to them, especially a parent, will die. Having an opportunity to talk about death and to learn about what we as Catholics believe about our hope for the future can be comforting for children this age. It also allows them to express their individual thoughts, questions, and fears.

CONSIDER THIS >>>

Do you think your child is a work in progress?

As human beings we grow emotionally, physically, and intellectually. We are also called to grow spiritually. We are moving ever toward the fullness of life God offers us in Heaven. "The Christian family forms an environment within which faith is professed and witnessed. When family members pray together, engage in lifelong learning, forgive one another, serve each other, welcome others, affirm and celebrate life, and bring justice and mercy to the community, they help each other live the faith and grow in faith" (*USCCA, p. 376*).

LET'S TALK >>>

- Talk about a time when you have needed comfort and the things others did to comfort you.
- Ask your child to name some reasons why Catholics look forward to the Second Coming of Christ.

LET'S PRAY >>>

 Saint Joseph, protect us as we live and watch over us at the end of our lives. Amen.

For a multimedia glossary of Catholic Faith Words, Sunday readings, seasonal and Saint resources, and chapter activities go to **aliveinchrist.osv.com**.

Chapter 21 Review

A **Work with Words** Complete each sentence with the correct word or words from the Word Bank.

Word Bank

Heaven

Hell

death

Last Judgment

Purgatory

1. Our earthly life will end in _____.

2. _____ is living with God forever.

3. A state of final cleansing after death and before entering Heaven is called _____.

4. Being separated from God forever because of human choice is called _____.

5. God's final triumph over evil, when Christ will come again to judge the living and the dead and bring the Kingdom of God to its fullness is called _____.

B **Check Understanding** Fill in the circle beside the correct answer.

6. You can comfort someone who is suffering a loss by _____.
   ○ ignoring them ○ telling jokes ○ going to the funeral

7. The _____ is the Catholic belief that Jesus will come again.
   ○ Holy Trinity ○ Second Coming ○ Lord's Prayer

8. Catholics look forward to _____ in God's Kingdom.
   ○ new life ○ big parties ○ eternal separation

9. God's grace and people's _____ will lead to everlasting life with God.
   ○ families ○ loving actions ○ good grades

10. John's vision of the end of time is called the Book of _____.
    ○ Mystery ○ Praise ○ Revelation

Go to **aliveinchrist.osv.com** for an interactive review.

A **Work with Words** Fill in the circle beside the correct answer.

1. A _____ is a sacred promise between God and humans.

   ○ vow   ○ covenant   ○ commitment

2. _____ is a state of cleansing before entering Heaven.

   ○ Purification   ○ Hell   ○ Purgatory

3. _____ is choosing to turn away from God and be separated from him forever.

   ○ Purgatory   ○ Hell   ○ Darkness

4. _____ is the virtue that moves people to give God and their neighbors what is their due.

   ○ Peace   ○ Charity   ○ Justice

5. _____ is the full joy of living with God forever.

   ○ Peace   ○ Justice   ○ Heaven

Write the letter T if the statement is TRUE. Write the letter F if the statement is FALSE.

6. ☐ Isaac made a covenant with God.

7. ☐ The work of the Church includes worshipping God, helping others know about the Holy Trinity, and working for peace and justice.

8. ☐ Giving witness means we sit by and watch what others do to help God build his Kingdom.

9. ☐ John had a vision of a new Heaven and Earth.

10. ☐ All faithful people will be raised to new life with God in Heaven.

B **Check Understanding** Circle the correct word to complete each sentence.

11. Early Christians remained _____ to God even when they were being persecuted.

faithful   **fearful**

12. Jesus and his early followers were _____.

Catholic   **Jewish**

13. God remained loyal to his covenant with the people of _____.

Egypt   **Israel**

14. Purgatory is a state of final _____ before entering Heaven.

judgment   **cleansing**

15. Basic human rights are food, clothing, shelter, and _____.

money   **dignity**

C **Make Connections** Complete each sentence with the correct word or words from the Word Bank.

16. Abraham's family grew to become the people

of _____.

17. To show by words or actions is to

_____.

18. _____ is a state of calm when people settle problems with kindness.

19. Our earthly lives will end in _____.

20. At the _____, God will triumph over evil and Christ will return to judge all the living and the dead.

Word Bank
Last Judgment
Israel
witness
death
peace

Write a response to each question or statement on the lines below.

21. How have you been a peacemaker?

_____

_____

_____

22. Give an example of a way that you could show solidarity.

_____

_____

_____

23. What does everlasting life mean?

_____

_____

_____

24. How are you preparing for the coming of God's Kingdom?

_____

_____

_____

25. How can you help keep the Church alive and growing?

_____

_____

_____

Life and Dignity

We read in the Bible that God knew us before we were even born: "Before I formed you...I knew you" (Jeremiah 1:5). God created each one of us. He has a plan for our lives. He knows what he made us to be.

Every life is valuable to God. Because God made each person, we should be kind and fair to everyone. We should take care of the bodies and minds God gave us and use them to do good things.

God wants us to be nice to others, and talk about problems instead of fighting. If we see someone else being mean, we should speak up, and get help if necessary. We should help to protect others because every life is important to God.

God wants you to treat each other with respect, even when you are upset.

Respect All People

At times, you might be tempted to think that people's value comes from how much money they have or the nice clothes they wear. When you think that, you are seeing as the world sees. God calls you to see as he sees!

When you see as God sees, you know that every human is a beloved child of God. Even when a person's actions make it hard to see God's goodness in him or her, that person is still created in God's image and is loved by God. Every Catholic is called by faith to respect all persons and to see the value in their lives.

≫ **How can you treat everyone you meet with dignity and respect?**

Share Life and Respect

God wants you to treat everyone fairly and with respect. He also wants all people to live happy, healthy lives. Place a heart next to the things that are needed for life. Place a star next to things you can do to show respect for other people.

Life	Respect
☐ lots of candy and treats	☐ be friendly and polite
☐ warm clothing	☐ ignore people you don't like
☐ good health	☐ laugh at people who are different
☐ a swimming pool	☐ share what you have

Call to Community

God gives us families and communities because he knows it would not be good for us to live our lives alone. In fact, the Bible says that this is why God created Eve to be a companion and friend to Adam, the first human being. (See Genesis 2:18.)

The Church teaches that God gives us families to help us learn who God is and how to love one another. Our parish community also helps us to learn about God. In families and in parish communities, we work together to take care of one another and to become the people God made us to be.

Live in Community

The one God in three Divine Persons (God the Father, God the Son, and God the Holy Spirit) is a communion of Divine love. God made humans to live in community. To teach people how to live in their first community—the family—God sent his own Son to live in a family with Mary and Joseph.

Catholics are called by their faith to participate in family life. Each time a family member acts with love, the family grows stronger. Each time a person shares in community life, the community grows stronger.

≫ **How can you help your family and your community grow stronger?**

Improve Your Community

What would make a stronger, better community? Does your playground need cleaning? Does anyone need help with homework? Or maybe your school needs a new computer. As a group decide on one item or service that would help, and plan to make it a reality.

_____

_____

_____

_____

Rights and Responsibilities

Because God made every person, everyone has rights and responsibilities. Rights are the freedoms or things every person needs and should have. Responsibilities are our duties, or the things we must do.

Jesus said, "You shall love your neighbor as yourself" (Mark 12:31). Following this command means making sure everyone's rights are protected. We also have a responsibility to treat others well and work together for the good of everyone.

Basic Rights

Every person has human rights. These are the basic things that people need to live happy, healthy lives according to God's plan. All people should have a safe place to live, clean water, and enough food. All people should be treated fairly.

As followers of Jesus, Christians have a special responsibility. One of the most important jobs is helping when someone's human rights have been taken away. When Catholics help protect the rights of others, they are doing the work of Jesus.

≫ **Why are Christians responsible for the human rights of others?**

Show That You Are Jesus' Friend

Jesus showed you how to care for others. When you live as Jesus lived, you are acting with justice, forgiveness, and love. Draw one way you can act with love so that people know you are a friend of Jesus.

Option for the Poor

In Scripture, Jesus says that whatever we have done for people who are poor or needy, we have also done for him. (See Matthew 25:40.) We should treat people the same way we would treat Jesus himself. When people need food, drink, clothing, housing, or medical care, or when they are lonely, we should try extra hard to help.

Saint Rose of Lima said, "When we serve the poor and the sick, we serve Jesus." Our Church teaches that we should have special love and care for those who are poor and put their needs first. When we do this, God will bless us.

One way we can give our time to help others is to volunteer for an organization that helps those in need.

The Needs of Others

Jesus' actions showed that he loved and cared for people who were poor, sick, or lonely. Your mission is to help others by imitating his loving actions. But who needs your help most? Like Jesus, you are called to help those who are poor and in need.

The Catholic Church teaches its members to be responsible for everyone in need, especially those who are poor. Organized groups, such as the St. Vincent de Paul Society, care for the needs of those who are poor. Individual Catholics give money, volunteer their time, and pray for those in need.

≫ **What Church groups do you know about that serve those who are poor in your area?**

Saint Vincent de Paul

Start Helping

Make a list of those who need your help the most. Write one thing you can do to help.

1. _____

2. _____

3. _____

I can help by _____

_____

The Dignity of Work

The different jobs people have help them earn money to buy food and other things they need to live. Jobs also allow people to work together with God and his creation. Work is part of God's plan for people, and everyone should work, either in the home or in a job outside the home.

All adults should be able to have a job if they want one. Scripture teaches that workers should be treated fairly by their bosses. (See Deuteronomy 24:14.) They should be given fair pay for their work. (See Leviticus 19:13 and Deuteronomy 24:15.) If workers are unhappy, they should be able to talk about this and work things out together with their bosses.

Rights of Workers

Work is not just a way to make money. Through work each day, humans join in God's work of creation. All work and all workers have dignity and value.

Workers are not always treated with the dignity and respect they deserve. Some workers earn too little pay and work too many hours. Others work in places that have unsafe conditions.

The Catholic Church wants all workers to be treated with respect and dignity. All workers must earn enough money to take care of their families. All workers should be able to work in safe places.

≫ **How can you appreciate the work your family does?**

Value Your Own Work

Use the chart below to track how you value yourself as a worker and the work you do. In each space, write at least one way you brought dignity to the work you do in your daily life.

The Dignity of Work		
At Home	**At School**	**With Others**
_____	_____	_____
_____	_____	_____
_____	_____	_____
_____	_____	_____

Human Solidarity

People around the world are different in many ways. Our hair, eyes, and skin are many different colors. There are people who are rich, people who are poor, and people who are in-between. People believe many different things about how we should live.

But one way we are all alike is that God made us. We are one human family. (See Galatians 3:28.) God calls everyone to be his children. Because God made everyone, we should treat everyone with love, kindness, and fairness. In the Beatitudes, Jesus says, "Blessed are the peacemakers" (Matthew 5:9). Treating others fairly will help us to live in peace with one another.

The Human Family

About seven billion people live on Earth today. All of those people are brothers and sisters in the family of God. When your brothers and sisters on Earth have troubles, you should find ways to help them. Taking care of others in the world shows solidarity, which means friendship and unity with everyone God created.

You show solidarity when you help bring peace to others. Sometimes you work for peace in your own family and neighborhood. Sometimes you need to help people who live far away. Wherever help is needed, Jesus calls his followers to bring his peace.

≫ **How can you be a person of peace every day?**

Discover the World

You can learn about people around the world by reading books that share information about people and life in other places. Discover the names and authors of three such books and write them here.

_____

_____

_____

Combine your list with those of your classmates to make a Friends Around the World reading list. Read at least a few of these books during the school year or over the summer.

Care for Creation

God created the whole world—the Earth and sky, the mountains and deserts, and all of the plants, animals, and people. When God made these things, he called them "very good" (Genesis 1:31). God put people in charge of the "fish of the sea, the birds of the air, and all the living things that crawl on the earth" (Genesis 1:28). God wants us to enjoy and take care of everything he has made.

Our Church teaches us that God gave the plants and animals for the good of all people. We should work to take care of the plants and animals and the places where they live, so everyone can enjoy them now and in the future. We should also be kind to animals, because they are God's creatures.

A Good Steward

When you show God that you are grateful for creation, you are being a good steward, or caregiver, of creation. Here are some ways to show you care.

Be grateful for foods that come from the Earth. Apples, berries, corn, and other fruits and vegetables are gifts from the Earth that help keep people healthy. Care for other people. People are the most important part of creation. Use natural resources with care. The water you drink, the air you breathe, and the land used to grow food are needed for all life on Earth. Taking care of them and using them well shows that you are a good steward.

≫ **How do you already care for creation?**

Show Thanks and Care

Draw a thank you card to show God that you are thankful for the wonderful world he created. Include some ways that you will care for God's creation.

The Holy Trinity

There are three Persons in one God—God the Father, God the Son, and God the Holy Spirit. The word for three Persons in one God is Holy Trinity.

God the Father, First Divine Person of the Trinity

We honor God the Father as the creator of all that exists. The Church prays to God the Father. Jesus taught his followers that God was his Father and their Father, too. Jesus said to pray using the words, "Our Father, who art in Heaven."

God the Son, Second Divine Person of the Trinity

We honor Jesus, God the Son, as the Savior of all people. Jesus is God, and he also became human. Jesus is the Messiah, God's chosen one. Messiah is a Hebrew word that means "the anointed one" or "the one chosen by God." Jesus has been given many names and titles that tell something special about him or honor him. These include Christ, Savior, Lord, Lamb of God (Agnus Dei), Son of God, Son of Man, the Word, and the Suffering Servant.

God the Holy Spirit, Third Divine Person of the Trinity

We honor God the Holy Spirit as our Guide and Helper. The Holy Spirit supports and comforts us and helps us live holier lives. He unites the Church and makes her mission possible. The Church uses symbols to describe the Holy Spirit. A dove, a flame, and the wind are all symbols of the Holy Spirit.

The Church

The Church is the community of all baptized people who believe in God and follow Jesus. The word is often used for the Catholic Church because she traces our origins back to the Apostles. The word *church* comes from two different words. One means "a community called together." The other means "belonging to the Lord." The Church is also sometimes called the "People of God."

The Pope, cardinals, bishops and archbishops, pastors, and other priests lead and guide the followers of Christ.

Body of Christ

Another name for the Church is "The Body of Christ." This name shows that you are closely joined with others and with Jesus. Church members work together just as parts of the body work together. The Church's mission is to share with others the Good News of God's Kingdom.

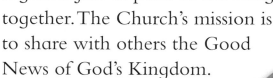

The Communion of Saints

All people living and dead who believe in Jesus and follow his way are part of the Communion of Saints. This includes people now alive on Earth and people who have died and are now in Purgatory or Heaven. People on Earth join in the Communion of Saints each time they celebrate the Eucharist.

Life After Death

The Church looks forward to the coming of God's Kingdom. When a Christian dies, he or she looks forward to the promise of a life forever with God. After people die, they will be in Heaven, Hell, or Purgatory.

- Heaven is the full joy of living with God forever.

- Hell is being separated from God forever because of a choice to turn away from him and not seek forgiveness.

- Purgatory is a preparation and final cleansing after death and before entering into Heaven. The word Purgatory means "making pure." Purgatory makes a person ready to be with God in Heaven.

Last Judgment

At the end of time, all Christians look forward to a time of happiness and peace. At that time Jesus will come again to judge the living and the dead. Then the Kingdom of God will come in fullness. The Church calls these events the Second Coming and the Last Judgment. These are times of hope and joy for Christians. Jesus' followers believe in the promise of God's everlasting Kingdom.

Marks of the Church

There are four Marks of the Church: one, holy, catholic, and apostolic. These essential characteristics identify Christ's Church and her mission.

1. The Church is one because the power of the Holy Spirit unites all of her members through one faith and one Baptism.

2. The Church is holy because she is set apart for God and his purposes. The Church shows God's holiness.

3. The Church is catholic because Jesus sent his followers out to tell the Good News to the whole world. The Church is universal, meant for all people in all times and places.

4. The Church is apostolic because she is built on the faith and leadership of the Apostles. Today the Church teaches directly from what the Apostles taught, and the bishops lead as the successors of the Apostles.

The Twelve Apostles

Peter	Philip	James, son of Alphaeus
James	Thomas	Simon the Zealot
John	Bartholomew	Judas
Andrew	Matthew	Matthias

Creeds

The Creed tells the faith of the Church. It brings together the Church's most important beliefs.

Apostles' Creed

This creed gives a summary of the Apostles' beliefs. It is often used at Mass during the season of Easter and in Masses with children. This creed is part of the Rosary.

I believe in God,
the Father almighty,
Creator of heaven and earth,
and in Jesus Christ, his only Son, our Lord,

At the words that follow, up to and including the Virgin Mary, all bow.

who was conceived by the Holy Spirit,
born of the Virgin Mary,
suffered under Pontius Pilate,
was crucified, died and was buried;
he descended into hell;
on the third day he rose again from the dead;
he ascended into heaven,
and is seated at the right hand
of God the Father almighty;
from there he will come to judge
the living and the dead.

I believe in the Holy Spirit,
the holy catholic Church,
the communion of saints,
the forgiveness of sins,
the resurrection of the body,
and life everlasting. Amen.

Nicene Creed

This creed was written over a thousand years ago by leaders of the Church who met at a city named Nicaea. Christians over the centuries have prayed. Today we pray this creed during most Masses.

I believe in one God,
the Father almighty,
maker of heaven and earth,
of all things visible and invisible.

I believe in one Lord Jesus Christ,
the Only Begotten Son of God,
born of the Father before all ages.
God from God, Light from Light,
true God from true God,
begotten, not made, consubstantial
    with the Father;
through him all things were made.
For us men and for our salvation
he came down from heaven,

*At the words that follow up to and including
and became man, all bow.*

and by the Holy Spirit was incarnate
    of the Virgin Mary, and became man.

For our sake he was crucified under
    Pontius Pilate,
he suffered death and was buried,
and rose again on the third day
in accordance with the Scriptures.

He ascended into heaven
and is seated at the right hand of
    the Father.
He will come again in glory
to judge the living and the dead
and his kingdom will have no end.

I believe in the Holy Spirit, the Lord,
    the giver of life,
who proceeds from the Father and
    the Son,
who with the Father and the Son is
    adored and glorified,
who has spoken through the prophets.

I believe in one, holy, catholic and
    apostolic Church.
I confess one Baptism for the
    forgiveness of sins
and I look forward to the resurrection
    of the dead
and the life of the world to come.
    Amen.

The Church Teaches

The Catholic Church uses several terms and titles when she speaks about her teaching. These ways of talking about the Church help all her members to be clear on what we believe and why. They will also be helpful to you in learning about the Church.

- A **doctrine** or **dogma** is an important teaching revealed by Christ and taught by the Church's Magisterium. As a Catholic, you are required to believe these revealed truths.

- An important ministry of the **Pope** and **bishops** is to teach with the guidance of the Holy Spirit. It is their duty to interpret the Catholic faith and explain it to all people.

- **Priests** and **deacons** assist the bishops in carrying out the teaching ministry. They do so by preaching, celebrating the Sacraments, and guiding the people.

- A **catechist** or **teacher** is someone who teaches the faith and helps people learn how to live according to the faith. Most catechists are laypeople. Religious sisters and brothers are often involved in this work of catechesis and education.

The Sanctuary of Our Lady of Fátima in Portugal

The Shrine to Our Lady of Lourdes in France

Mary

Mary is Jesus' Mother. For this reason she is called the Mother of God. The Church honors Mary because she was willing to do what God asked. Mary is a model for Christians of all times and places.

Titles of Mary

The Church honors Mary with many titles. Each tells something about her and why she is so loved. Mary is called the Immaculate Conception, the Blessed Virgin, the Madonna, Our Lady of Perpetual Help, Queen of Heaven, Help of Christians, the Morning Star, and Queen of Angels.

Many Christians honor Mary by naming their children after her. Mary, Marie, and Maria are forms of the name you may know. Marilyn, Maureen, Moira, Marianne, and Marita are some of the names that mean "Mary" in other languages.

The name Madonna means "my lady" in Italian. Regina means "queen" in Latin. And Virginia is a name that refers to Mary's virginity. In Spanish-speaking countries children are also named Lupe (for Our Lady of Guadalupe), Concepción (for the Immaculate Conception), Dolores (for Our Lady of Sorrows), or Gracia (for Our Lady of Grace).

The Seven Sacraments

Catholics share in the worship of the Church by participating in the Seven Sacraments. The Sacraments are special signs and celebrations that Jesus gave his Church. They allow us to share in God's life and work. The Sacraments are divided into three groups.

The Mass

The Mass is the celebration of the Sacrament of the Eucharist. The Mass includes two main parts: the Liturgy of the Word and the Liturgy of the Eucharist.

At the Liturgy of the Word you listen to readings from Scripture. The priest gives a homily. He explains the readings and how they apply to our lives. We all profess our faith by saying one of the creeds.

The Liturgy of the Eucharist includes prayers and songs thanking and praising God, and offering the gifts of bread and wine. Then the priest blesses the bread and wine, which become the Body and Blood of Christ. Those gathered pray the Lord's Prayer and give one another a sign of peace. This shows they are ready to come to the Lord's table. The people share in Jesus' sacrifice when they receive Holy Communion.

When the Mass ends, those gathered are sent to "Go and announce the Gospel of the Lord" in their own community.

The Seven Sacraments

Sacraments of Initiation	
The three Sacraments that celebrate membership into the Catholic Church.	• Baptism • Confirmation • Eucharist

Sacraments of Healing	
In these Sacraments, God's forgiveness and healing are given to those suffering physical and spiritual sickness.	• Penance and Reconciliation • Anointing of the Sick

Sacraments at the Service of Communion	
These Sacraments celebrate people's commitment to serve God and the community and help build up the People of God.	• Holy Orders • Matrimony (Marriage)

© Our Sunday Visitor

Order of Mass

The Mass follows a pattern, with some differences according to the feast or season of the liturgical year. The main parts of the Mass are the Liturgy of the Word and the Liturgy of the Eucharist.

The Order of Mass

Introductory Rites

1. Entrance Chant
2. Greeting
3. Rite for the Blessing and Sprinkling of Water
4. Penitential Act
5. Kyrie
6. Gloria
7. Collect

Liturgy of the Word

1. First Reading (usually from the Old Testament)
2. Responsorial Psalm
3. Second Reading (from the New Testament letters)
4. Gospel Acclamation (Alleluia)
5. Gospel Dialogue
6. Gospel Reading
7. Homily
8. Profession of Faith (Creed)
9. Prayer of the Faithful

Liturgy of the Eucharist

1. Preparation of the Gifts
2. Invitation to Prayer
3. Prayer over the Offerings
4. Eucharistic Prayer
   - Preface Dialogue
   - Preface
   - Preface Acclamation
   - Consecration
   - Mystery of Faith
   - Concluding Doxology
5. Communion Rite
   - The Lord's Prayer
   - Sign of Peace
   - Lamb of God (Agnus Dei)
   - Invitation to Communion
   - Communion
   - Prayer after Communion

Concluding Rites

1. Greeting
2. Blessing
3. Dismissal

Special Church Objects

 **Altar** the central table at the front of the church where the Eucharist is celebrated.

 Ambo (lectern) the place where Scripture is proclaimed and homilies preached. The lector (reader), deacon, and priest stand behind the lectern to announce God's Word.

 Baptismal Font/Pool the container that holds blessed holy water for celebrating Baptisms.

 Tabernacle the special place in the church where the Blessed Sacrament is reserved after Mass for those who are ill or for Eucharistic Adoration.

 **Book of Gospels** the special book that contains the Gospel readings used at Mass.

 Chalice the cup for the Blood of Christ.

 Ciborium the special container placed in the Tabernacle that holds the Eucharistic Hosts, the Body of Christ.

 Lectionary the special book used at Mass that contains readings from the Old and New Testament.

 **Paschal Candle** a large, decorated candle that is lit from the new fire at the Easter Vigil. This candle is lit at all masses during the Easter season. It is also lit at Baptisms and funerals.

 **Roman Missal** the special book that contains the prayers of the Mass.

© Our Sunday Visitor

Liturgical Colors

Certain colors are used during certain seasons of the Church year. These colors are used for parts of the priest's vestments.

Colors	
Green	Sundays in Ordinary Time
Red	Palm Sunday, Good Friday, Pentecost
Rose	Third Sunday of Advent and Fourth Sunday of Lent
Purple or Violet	Advent and Lent
White	Christmas, Easter, Feasts of the Lord, Mary, and the Saints not martyred, or funerals

Sacramentals

As a reminder of Jesus' presence, the Church uses special signs and symbols. They are called sacramentals. A sacramental can be an object, words, gesture, or action. They are made sacred through the prayers of the Church.

Sacramentals often include an action like the Sign of the Cross. Crucifixes, holy cards, and medals remind you of Jesus, the Blessed Mother, or the Saints.

Palm branches remind you of Jesus' entry into Jerusalem. After the Palm Sunday service, you can keep and display the palm branches in your home. These are all popular sacramentals.

Blessings

A blessing is a special sign and prayer. Blessings praise God. They ask for God's care for a person, a place, a thing, or an action. In many churches on the feast day of Saint Francis of Assisi (October 4), the priest blesses pets or farm animals.

Devotions

Devotions are special prayers that honor God, Mary, or the Saints. Visits to the Blessed Sacrament are a popular devotion to honor Jesus. The Rosary is a devotion to honor Mary. Devotions help people remember to pray outside of Mass.

God's Laws

God desires you to be in relationship with him. To help you do this and to know what is right, he has given you laws.

The Ten Commandments

	The Ten Commandments	Their Meaning
1	I am the Lord your God: you shall not have strange gods before me.	Keep God first in your life.
2	You shall not take the name of the Lord your God in vain.	Always use God's name in a reverent way.
3	Remember to keep holy the Lord's Day.	Attend Mass and rest on Sunday.
4	Honor your father and your mother.	Obey your parents and guardians.
5	You shall not kill.	Be kind to the people and animals God made; care for yourself and others.
6	You shall not commit adultery.	Be respectful in the things you do with your body.
7	You shall not steal.	Take care of other people's things; don't take what belongs to someone else. Respect other people and their property.
8	You shall not bear false witness against your neighbor.	Respect others by always telling the truth.
9	You shall not covet your neighbor's wife.	Keep your thoughts and words clean; don't be jealous of other people's friendships.
10	You shall not covet your neighbor's goods.	Be happy with the things you have; don't be jealous of what other people have.

The Great Commandment

[Jesus] said in reply, "You shall love the Lord, your God, with all your heart, with all your being, with all your strength, and with all your mind, and your neighbor as yourself." Luke 10:27

The Beatitudes

Blessed are the poor in spirit,
for theirs is the kingdom of heaven.
Blessed are they who mourn,
for they will be comforted.
Blessed are the meek,
for they will inherit the land.
Blessed are they who hunger and thirst
   for righteousness,
for they will be satisfied.
Blessed are the merciful,
for they will be shown mercy.
Blessed are the clean of heart,
for they will see God.
Blessed are the peacemakers,
for they will be called children of God.
Blessed are they who are persecuted for
   the sake of righteousness,
for theirs is the kingdom of heaven.
Matthew 5:3–10

Jesus' New Commandment

Jesus also gave his followers a New Commandment: "love one another. As I have loved you, so you also should love one another." John 13:34

Corporal and Spiritual Works of Mercy

The Corporal Works of Mercy draw Catholics to the care of the physical needs of others. The Spiritual Works of Mercy guide us to care for the spiritual needs of people.

Corporal

- Feed the hungry
- Give drink to the thirsty
- Clothe the naked
- Shelter the homeless
- Visit the sick
- Visit the imprisoned

Spiritual

- Warn the sinner
- Teach the ignorant
- Counsel the doubtful
- Comfort the sorrowful
- Bear wrongs patiently
- Forgive injuries
- Pray for the living and the dead

Virtue

The word virtue means "strength." Virtues are good spiritual habits that make you stronger and help you do what is right and good. Practicing these habits of goodness helps you to make even more loving choices.

The Theological Virtues

These three virtues are gifts from God.

Faith—Faith makes it possible to believe in God and all that he has shown us. Faith leads you to obey God and all he has taught.

Hope—Hope is the virtue that helps you trust in what God has shown you. It is the gift of looking forward to the happiness of life forever with God and the coming of God's Kingdom.

Charity (Love)—You show your love for God by praising him and making him number one in your life. You also show love for God by loving other people and by treating everyone with kindness and respect. You help people. You listen to friends who have problems. You do kind things.

Cardinal Virtues

These are the four principle moral virtues that help us live as children of God and from which the other moral virtues flow. We strengthen these good habits through God's grace and our own efforts.

Prudence—being practical and making correct decisions on what is right and good, with the help of the Holy Spirit and a formed conscience.

Justice—giving God what is due him. It also means to give each person what he or she is due because that person is a child of God.

Fortitude—showing courage, having strength to get through difficult times, not giving up when doing good.

Temperance—using moderation, being disciplined, and

Precepts of the Church

The following precepts are important duties of all Catholics.

1. Take part in Mass on Sundays and holy days. Keep these days holy and avoid unnecessary work.

2. Celebrate the Sacrament of Reconciliation at least once a year.

3. Receive Holy Communion at least once a year during the Easter season.

4. Fast and abstain on days of penance.

5. Give your time, gifts, and money to support the Church.

Gifts of the Holy Spirit

You receive the Gifts of the Holy Spirit through the Sacraments of Baptism and Confirmation. These gifts help you grow in relationship with God and others.

- Wisdom
- Understanding
- Right Judgment (Counsel)
- Courage (Fortitude)
- Knowledge
- Reverence (Piety)
- Wonder and Awe (Fear of the Lord)

Examination of Conscience

1. Pray to the Holy Spirit to help you examine your conscience.

2. Read the Beatitudes, the Ten Commandments, the Great Commandment, and the Precepts of the Church.

3. Ask yourself these questions:

- When have I not done what God wants me to do?
- Whom have I hurt?
- What have I done that I knew was wrong?
- What have I not done that I should have done?
- Have I done penance and tried to change?
- With what am I still having trouble?
- Am I sorry for all my sins?

Basic Prayers

These are essential prayers that every Catholic should know. Latin is the official, universal language of the Church. As members of the Catholic Church, we usually pray in the language that we speak, but we sometimes pray in Latin, the common language of the Church.

Sign of the Cross

In the name of the Father,
and of the Son,
and of the Holy Spirit.
Amen.

Signum Crucis

In nómine Patris
et Fílii
et Spíritus Sancti.
Amen.

The Lord's Prayer

Our Father, who art in heaven,
hallowed be thy name;
thy kingdom come,
thy will be done
on earth as it is in heaven.
Give us this day our daily bread,
and forgive us our trespasses,
as we forgive those who trespass
 against us;
and lead us not into temptation,
but deliver us from evil. Amen.

Pater Noster

Pater noster qui es in cælis:
santificétur Nomen Tuum;
advéniat Regnum Tuum;
fiat volúntas Tua,
sicut in cælo, et in terra.
Panem nostrum
cotidiánum da nobis hódie;
et dimítte nobis débita nostra,
sicut et nos
dimíttus debitóribus nostris;
et ne nos indúcas in tentatiónem;
sed líbera nos a Malo.

Glory Be

Glory be to the Father
and to the Son
and to the Holy Spirit,
as it was in the beginning
is now, and ever shall be
world without end. Amen.

Gloria Patri

Gloria Patri
et Fílio
et Spíritui Sancto.
Sicut erat in princípio,
et nunc et semper
et in sǽcula sǽculorem. Amen.

The Hail Mary

Hail, Mary, full of grace,
the Lord is with thee.
Blessed art thou among women
and blessed is the fruit of thy womb,
  Jesus.
Holy Mary, Mother of God,
pray for us sinners,
now and at the hour of our death.
Amen.

Ave Maria

Ave, María, grátia plena,
Dóminus tecum.
Benedícta tu in muliéribus,
et benedíctus fructus ventris
  tui, Iesus.
Sancta María, Mater Dei,
ora pro nobis peccatóribus,
nunc et in hora mortis nostræ.
Amen.

Prayers from the Sacraments

I Confess/*Confiteor*

I confess to almighty God
and to you, my brothers and sisters,
that I have greatly sinned,
in my thoughts and in my words,
in what I have done and in what I have
failed to do,

Gently strike your chest with a closed fist.

through my fault, through my fault,
through my most grievous fault;

Continue:

therefore I ask blessed Mary ever-Virgin,
all the Angels and Saints,
and you, my brothers and sisters,
to pray for me to the Lord our God.

The Apostles' Creed

See page 308 for this prayer.

The Nicene Creed

See page 309 for this prayer.

Gloria

Glory to God in the highest,
and on earth peace to people of
good will.

We praise you, we bless you, we adore
you, we glorify you, we give you
thanks for your great glory,
Lord God, heavenly King, O God,
almighty Father.

Lord Jesus Christ,
Only Begotten Son,
Lord God, Lamb of God,
Son of the Father,
you take away the sins of the world,
have mercy on us;
you take away the sins of the world,
receive our prayer;
you are seated at the right hand of
the Father, have mercy on us.

For you alone are the Holy One,
you alone are the Lord,
you alone are the Most High,
Jesus Christ, with the Holy Spirit,
in the glory of God the Father.
Amen.

Holy, Holy, Holy Lord

Holy, Holy, Holy Lord God of hosts.
Heaven and earth are full of your glory.
Hosanna in the highest.
Blessed is he who comes in the name of
the Lord.
Hosanna in the highest.

Lamb of God

Lamb of God, you take away the
sins of the world,
have mercy on us.
Lamb of God, you take away the
sins of the world,
have mercy on us.
Lamb of God, you take away the
sins of the world,
grant us peace.

Prayer to the Holy Spirit

Come, Holy Spirit, fill the hearts of your
faithful.
And kindle in them the fire of your love.
Send forth your Spirit and they shall be
created.
And you will renew the face of the
earth.

Act of Contrition

(From Rite of Penance)
*Often used at night after a brief
examination of conscience.*
My God, I am sorry for my sins
with all my heart.
In choosing to do wrong
and failing to do good,
I have sinned against you
whom I should love above all things.
I firmly intend, with your help,
to do penance, to sin no more,
and to avoid whatever leads me to sin.
Our Savior Jesus Christ
suffered and died for us.
In his name, my God, have mercy.

Personal and Family Prayers

Daily Prayer

We begin each day and end each day with prayer. That is because we want him to guide all that we say and do. We ask him to be with us as we go about our day. We then thank him for everything he does and gives, asking him to be with us as we sleep.

Grace Before Meals

Bless us, O Lord, and these thy gifts which we are about to receive from thy bounty, through Christ our Lord. Amen.

Grace After Meals

We give you thanks, Almighty God, for all these gifts which we have received from thy bounty, through Christ our Lord. Amen.

Morning Prayer

Blessed are you, Lord, God of all creation: you take the sleep from my eyes and the slumber from my eyelids. Amen.

Morning Offering

Almighty God, we thank you for the life and light of a new day. Keep us safe today and protect us from every evil. We offer ourselves this day to you through Jesus Christ your Son. May your Holy Spirit make our thoughts, words, and actions pleasing in your sight. Amen.

Evening Prayer

Protect us, Lord, as we stay awake; watch over us as we sleep, that awake, we may keep watch with Christ, and asleep, rest in his peace. Amen.

Angel Guardian

An angel is a spiritual being that is a messenger of God. Angels are mentioned nearly 300 times in the Bible.

Three important angels are Gabriel, Michael, and Raphael.

Traditional

Angel of God,
my Guardian dear,
to whom God's love commits
me here.
Ever this day (night)
be at my side,
to light and guard,
to rule and guide.

Contemporary

Angel sent by God to guide me,
be my light and walk beside me;
be my guardian and protect me;
on the paths of life direct me.

Act of Faith, Hope, and Love

Often prayed in the morning to remind us that all gifts come from God, and that he can help us believe, trust, and love.

My God, I believe in you,
I trust in you,
I love you above all things,
with all my heart and mind and
strength.
I love you because you are supremely
good and
worth loving;
and because I love you,
I am sorry with all my heart for
offending you.
Lord, have mercy on me, a sinner.
Amen.

Act of Contrition

Often used at night after a brief examination of conscience.
See page 323 for this prayer.

Praying with the Saints

When we pray with the Saints, we ask them to pray to God for us and to pray with us. The Saints are with Christ. They speak for us when we need help.

As the Mother of Jesus, the Son of God, Mary is called the Mother of God, the Queen of all Saints, and the Mother of the Church. There are many prayers and practices of devotion to Mary.

Angelus

The Angelus is a prayer honoring the Incarnation. It is given its name by the first word of the Latin version of the prayer: Angelus Domini nuntiavit Maria, "The angel of the Lord declared unto Mary." To honor the Incarnation, it is recited three times each day—morning, noon, and evening, at the sound of the Angelus bell. Each response, where shown, is followed by reciting the Hail Mary.

V. The angel spoke God's message to Mary,
R. and she conceived of the Holy Spirit.
Hail, Mary,…

V. "I am the lowly servant of the Lord:
R. let it be done to me according to your word."

Hail, Mary,…
V. And the Word became flesh,
R. and lived among us.
Hail, Mary,…
V. Pray for us, holy Mother of God,
R. that we may become worthy of the promises of Christ.
Let us pray.

Lord,
fill our hearts with your grace:
once, through the message of an angel you revealed to us the Incarnation of your Son;
now, through his suffering and death lead us to the glory of his resurrection.

We ask this through Christ our Lord. Amen.

The Rosary

One of the most popular prayers is the Rosary. It focuses on the twenty mysteries that describe the events in the lives of Jesus and Mary.

How to Pray the Rosary

1. Pray the Sign of the Cross and say the Apostles' Creed.

2. Pray the Lord's Prayer.

3. Pray three Hail Marys.

4. Pray the Glory Be to the Father.

5. Say the first mystery; then pray the Lord's Prayer.

6. Pray ten Hail Marys while meditating on the mystery.

7. Pray the Glory Be to the Father.

8. Say the second mystery; then pray the Lord's Prayer. Repeat 6 and 7 and continue with the third, fourth, and fifth mysteries in the same manner.

9. Pray the Hail, Holy Queen.

Hail, Holy Queen

Hail, Holy Queen, Mother of Mercy,
our life, our sweetness, and
    our hope.
To you do we cry,
poor banished children of Eve.
To you do we send up our sighs,
mourning and weeping in this valley
    of tears.
Turn then, most gracious advocate,
your eyes of mercy toward us,
and after this exile
show unto us the blessed fruit of thy
    womb, Jesus.
O clement, O loving,
O sweet Virgin Mary.

The Mysteries of the Rosary

The Joyful Mysteries
The Annunciation
The Visitation
The Nativity
The Presentation in the Temple
The Finding in the Temple

The Luminous Mysteries
The Baptism of Jesus
The Wedding at Cana
The Proclamation of the Kingdom
The Transfiguration
The Institution of the Eucharist

The Sorrowful Mysteries
The Agony in the Garden
The Scourging at the Pillar
The Crowning with Thorns
The Carrying of the Cross
The Crucifixion and Death

The Glorious Mysteries
The Resurrection
The Ascension
The Descent of the Holy Spirit
The Assumption of Mary
The Coronation of Mary in Heaven

Catholic Faith Words

Apostles' Creed one of the Church's oldest creeds. It is a summary of Christian beliefs taught since the time of the Apostles. This creed is used in the celebration of Baptism. (90)

apostolic the teaching authority of the Church comes directly from Jesus and his chosen Apostles because the bishops of the Church are direct successors of the Apostles; a Mark of the Church (167)

Apostolic Succession the term used to describe how the authority and power to lead and teach the Church is passed down from the Apostles to their successors, the bishops (158)

Ascension when the Risen Jesus was taken up to Heaven to be with God the Father forever (135)

Beatitudes teachings of Jesus that show the way to true happiness and tell how to live in God's Kingdom now and always (193)

Bible the Word of God written in human words. The Bible is the holy book of the Church. (65)

bishop an ordained man who works together with other bishops and the Pope in teaching, leading, and making the Church holy. The bishops are the successors of the Apostles. (158)

Blessed Sacrament a name for the Holy Eucharist, especially the Body of Christ kept in the Tabernacle (101)

blessing and adoration in this prayer form, we show that we understand God is the Creator of all and that we need him. We give him respect and honor his greatness. (111)

Body of Christ a name for the Church of which Christ is the head. All the baptized are members of the body. (142)

catholic the Church is meant for all people in all times and all places; a Mark of the Church (167)

charity the theological virtue of love. It directs us to love God above all things and our neighbor as ourselves, for the love of God. (203)

Church the community of all baptized people who believe in God and follow Jesus. The word is often used for the Catholic Church because we trace our origins back to the Apostles. (67)

© Our Sunday Visitor

Communion of Saints everyone who believes in and follows Jesus—people on Earth and people who have died and are in Purgatory or Heaven **(169)**

conscience an ability given to us by God that helps us make choices about right and wrong **(210)**

covenant a sacred promise or agreement between God and humans **(258)**

creation everything made by God **(55)**

creed a statement of the Church's beliefs **(90)**

deacon an ordained man who serves the Church by assisting in the Eucharist, baptizing, witnessing marriages, and doing works of charity **(245)**

domestic Church a name for the Catholic family, because it is the community of Christians in the home. God made the family to be the first place we learn about loving others and following Christ. **(76)**

E–G

Eucharist the Sacrament in which Jesus shares himself, and the bread and wine become his Body and Blood **(226)**

evangelization sharing the Good News of Jesus through words and actions in a way that invites people to accept the Gospel **(178)**

faith the theological virtue that makes it possible for us to believe in God and all that he helps us understand about himself. Faith leads us to obey God. **(202)**

faithful to be constant and loyal to your promises and commitments to God and others, just as he is faithful to you **(260)**

Gospel a word that means "Good News." The Gospel message is the Good News of God's Kingdom and his saving love. **(122)**

grace God's free and loving gift to humans of his own life and help **(210)**

Heaven the full joy of living with God forever **(280)**

Hell being separated from God forever because of a choice to turn away from him and not seek forgiveness **(280)**

holy the Church is holy because she is set apart for God and his purposes; a Mark of the Church **(167)**

Holy Trinity the one God in three Divine Persons—God the Father, God the Son, and God the Holy Spirit **(57)**

hope the theological virtue that helps us trust in the true happiness God wants us to have and in Jesus' promises of eternal life, and to rely on the help of the Holy Spirit **(203)**

© Our Sunday Visitor

I–K

image of God the likeness of God that is in all human beings because we are created by him (57)

Incarnation the mystery that the Son of God became man to save all people (88)

intercession in this prayer form, we ask God to help others (111)

justice giving God what is due him, and giving each person what he or she is due because that person is a child of God (271)

Kingdom of God the world of love, peace, and justice that is in Heaven and is still being built on Earth (124)

L–M

Last Judgment God's final triumph over evil that will occur at the end of time, when Christ returns and judges all the living and the dead (280)

Last Supper the meal Jesus shared with his disciples on the night before he died. At the Last Supper, Jesus gave himself in the Eucharist. (98)

liturgy the public prayer of the Church. It includes the Sacraments and forms of daily prayer. (100)

Lord's Prayer the prayer that Jesus taught his disciples to pray to God the Father (108)

Magisterium the teaching office of the Church, which is all of the bishops in union with the Pope (159)

Marks of the Church the four characteristics that identify Christ's Church: one, holy, catholic, and apostolic (167)

Mary the Mother of Jesus, the Mother of God. She is also called "Our Lady" because she is our Mother and the Mother of the Church. (74)

mercy kindness and concern for those who are suffering. God has mercy on us even though we are sinners. (193)

Messiah the promised one who would lead his People. The word Messiah means "God's anointed," or "God's chosen one." Jesus is the Messiah. (123)

miracle something that cannot be explained by science, but happened by the power of God (124)

mission a job or purpose. The Church's mission is to announce the Good News of God's Kingdom. (178)

missionaries people who answer God's call to bring the message of Jesus and announce the Good News of his Kingdom to people in other places (178)

mystery a spiritual truth that is difficult to perceive or understand with our senses, but is known through faith and through signs (88)

N–P

New Commandment Jesus' command for his disciples to love one another as he has loved us (193)

Nicene Creed a summary of basic beliefs about God the Father, God the Son, and God the Holy Spirit and about other Church teachings. We usually say the Nicene Creed during Mass. (100)

one the Church is one because the power of the Holy Spirit unites all the members through one faith and one Baptism; a mark of the Church (167)

parable a short story Jesus told about everyday life to teach something about God (125)

parish the local community of Catholics that meets at a particular place (142)

Paschal Mystery the mystery of Jesus' suffering, Death, Resurrection, and Ascension (135)

peace a state of calm when things are in their proper order and people settle problems with kindness and justice (271)

Pentecost the feast that celebrates the coming of the Holy Spirit fifty days after Easter (168)

petition in this prayer form, we ask God for what we need (111)

Pope the successor of Peter, the bishop of Rome, and the head of the entire Church (157)

praise in this prayer form, we give God honor and thanks because he is God (111)

prayer talking and listening to God. It is raising your mind and heart to God. (108)

Precepts of the Church some of the minimum requirements given by Church leaders for deepening our relationship with God and the Church (210)

priest an ordained man who helps his bishop by leading a parish, preaching the Gospel, and celebrating the Eucharist and other Sacraments (245)

proclaim to tell about Jesus in words and actions (258)

Purgatory a state of final cleansing after death and before entering into Heaven (280)

R–S

Real Presence the teaching that Jesus is really and truly with us in the Eucharist. We receive Jesus in his fullness. (226)

Resurrection the event of Jesus being raised from Death to new life by God the Father through the power of the Holy Spirit (134)

Sacraments at the Service of Communion the two Sacraments that celebrate people's commitment to serve God and the community: Holy Orders and Matrimony (246)

Sacraments of Healing Penance and Reconciliation and the Anointing of the Sick. In these Sacraments, God's forgiveness and healing are given to those suffering physical and spiritual sickness. **(236)**

Sacraments of Initiation the three Sacraments that celebrate membership into the Catholic Church: Baptism, Confirmation, and Eucharist **(226)**

Sacred Chrism perfumed oil used for the Sacraments of Baptism, Confirmation, and Holy Orders **(224)**

Sacred Tradition God's Word handed down verbally through the Apostles and bishops **(67)**

sacrifice giving up something out of love for someone else or for the common good (the good of everyone). Jesus sacrificed his life for all people. **(132)**

Saint a hero of the Church who loved God very much, led a holy life, and is now with God in Heaven **(169)**

Seven Sacraments special signs and celebrations that Jesus gave his Church. The Sacraments allow us to share in the life and work of God. **(98)**

sin a person's choice to disobey God on purpose and do what he or she knows is wrong. Sins hurt our relationship with God and other people. **(213)**

stewardship the way we appreciate and use God's gifts, including our time, talent, and treasure and the resources of creation **(145)**

T–V

Tabernacle the special place in the church where the Blessed Sacrament is reserved after Mass for those who are ill or for Eucharistic Adoration **(101)**

thanksgiving in this prayer form, we give thanks to God for all he has given us **(111)**

Theological Virtues the virtues of faith, hope, and charity (love), which are gifts from God that guide our relationship with him **(202)**

virtues good spiritual habits that make you stronger and help you do what is right and good. They grow over time with our practice and openness to God's grace. **(202)**

Visitation the name of Mary's visit to Elizabeth before Jesus was born **(74)**

vocation God's plan for our lives; the purpose for which he made us **(201)**

vows solemn promises that are made to or before God **(244)**

Index

Index

Photo Credits:

v Mike Kemp/Tetra Images/Corbis; vi Bill & Peggy Wittman; viii Elio Ciol/Corbis; 1 Jupiterimages/Polka Dot/Thinkstock; 2 Alex Mares-Manton/Picture India/Corbis; 3 Bill & Peggy Wittman; 4 iStockphoto/Thinkstock; 6 Our Sunday Visitor; 7 (bg) Image Copyright Joan Kerrigan, 2013 Used under license from Shutterstock.com; 7 (inset) The Crosiers/Gene Plaisted, OSC; 9 Bill & Peggy Wittman; 10 Robert Harding Picture Library Ltd/Alamy; 11 (t) The Crosiers/Gene Plaisted, OSC; 11 (b) Bill & Peggy Wittman; 13 Image Copyright Philip Meyer, 2012 Used under license from Shutterstock.com; 14 (l) Robert Harding Picture Library Ltd/Alamy; 14 (r) Bill & Peggy Wittman; 16 Bill & Peggy Wittman; 17 Image Copyright Philip Meyer, 2012 Used under license from Shutterstock.com; 18 Chad Ehlers/Alamy; 19 Bill & Peggy Wittman; 22 (l) Bill & Peggy Wittman; 22 (r) Bill & Peggy Wittman; 24 Cerri, Lara/ZUMA Press/Corbis; 25 Chip Somodevilla/Getty Images; 26-27 Image Copyright Philip Meyer, 2012 Used under license from Shutterstock.com; 28 (l) Chip Somodevilla/Getty Images; 28 (r) iStockphoto.com/DNY59; 29 Our Sunday Visitor; 30 Veronique DUPONT/AFP/Getty Images; 31 Con Tanasiuk/Design Pics/Corbis; 32–33 Image Copyright Philip Meyer, 2012 Used under license from Shutterstock.com; 34 (l) Veronique DUPONT/AFP/Getty Images; 34 (r) The Annunciation, c.1623 (oil on canvas) (detail of 59265), Gentileschi, Orazio (1565-1647)/Galleria Sabauda, Turin, Italy/The Bridgeman Art Library; 35 Bill & Peggy Wittman; 36 Bill & Peggy Wittman; 37 Image Copyright Philip Meyer, 2012 Used under license from Shutterstock.com; 38 (l) Bill & Peggy Wittman; 38 (r) Bill & Peggy Wittman; 39 iStockphoto/Thinkstock; 40 Bill & Peggy Wittman; 41 Providence Collection/Licensed From Goodsalt.com; 42–43 Image Copyright Philip Meyer, 2012 Used under license from Shutterstock.com; 44 (l) Providence Collection/Licensed From Goodsalt.com; 44 (r) The Ascension, left hand panel from the Altarpiece, c.1466 (tempera on panel) (see also 50042), Mantegna, Andrea (1431–1506)/Galleria degli Uffizi, Florence, Italy/Alinari/The Bridgeman Art Library; 45 deleting-folder/Alamy; 46 Florian Kopp/imagebro/age fotostock; 48–49 Image Copyright Philip Meyer, 2012 Used under license from Shutterstock.com; 50 (l) deleting-folder/Alamy; 50 (r) Bill & Peggy Wittman; 52 (c) WALTER ZERLA/cultura/Corbis; 52 (b) Ron Nickel/Design Pics/Corbis; 53 Hill Street Studios/Blend Images/Corbis; 54 (c) iStockphoto/Thinkstock; 54 (b) Digital Vision/Thinkstock; 55 (l) Image Source/Corbis; 55 (c) Winfried Wisniewski/Corbis; 55 (r) Peter Frank/Corbis; 57 Blend Images/SuperStock; 58 Photodisc/Getty Images; 59 Tetra Images/Corbis; 60 (bg) Image Copyright Joan Kerrigan, 2013 Used under license from Shutterstock.com; 60 (inset) Jim Hughes/Corbis; 63 Bill & Peggy Wittman; 64 (bg) SuperStock/Glowimages; 64 (inset) Photographe: Frère Denis, c.s.c./AFP/Getty Images; 65 Providence Collection/Licensed From Goodsalt.com; 66 Bill & Peggy Wittman; 68 (t) Cultura Creative/Alamy; 68 (b) Deborah Jaffe/Corbis; 70 Image Copyright Joan Kerrigan, 2013 Used under license from Shutterstock.com; 71 Bill & Peggy Wittman; 75 Bill & Peggy Wittman; 76 Jose Luis Pelaez, Inc./Blend Images/Corbis; 77 Ocean/Corbis; 78 Martin Rügner/Westend61/Corbis; 80 Image Copyright Joan Kerrigan, 2013 Used under license from Shutterstock.com; 81 Jose Luis Pelaez, Inc./Blend Images/Corbis; 86 (c) Frank Krahmer/StockImage/Alamy; 86 (b) iStockphoto.com/patty_c ; 87 (bg) Jim Whitmer; 87 (inset) The Crosiers/Gene Plaisted, OSC; 90 Ocean/Corbis; 91 Our Sunday Visitor; 92 Birgid Allig/Corbis; 94 (bg) Image Copyright Joan Kerrigan, 2013 Used under license from Shutterstock.com; 94 (inset) Ocean/Corbis; 95 Ocean/Corbis; 99 Bill & Peggy Wittman; 100 Bill & Peggy Wittman; 101 Bill & Peggy Wittman; 102 Our Sunday Visitor; 104 (bg) Image Copyright Joan Kerrigan, 2013 Used under license from Shutterstock.com; 104 (inset) Bill & Peggy Wittman; 105 Bill & Peggy Wittman; 107 (t) Myrleen Pearson/PhotoEdit; 107 (bl) Kyu Oh/Photodisc/Getty Images; 107 (br) Our Sunday Visitor; 108 Justinen Creative/Licensed From Goodsalt.com; 110 Mike Kemp/Tetra Images/Corbis; 111 Bill & Peggy Wittman; 112 (t) Brand X Pictures/Thinkstock; 112 (b) Push Pictures/Corbis; 114 (bg) Image Copyright Joan Kerrigan, 2013 Used under license from Shutterstock.com; 114 (inset) Top Photo Group/Thinkstock; 115 Brand X Pictures/Thinkstock; 120 (c) Simon Jarratt/Corbis; 120 (b) Standard Publishing/Licensed From Goodsalt.com; 122 Blend Images/Alamy; 123 Lars Justinen/Licensed From Goodsalt.com; 124 Jim Whitmer; 128 (bg) Image Copyright SergiyN, 2012 Used under license from Shutterstock.com; 128 (inset) Bill & Peggy Wittman; 131 Ken Seet/Corbis; 133 Bill & Peggy Wittman; 135 Bill & Peggy Wittman; 136 (t) Blue Images/Corbis; 136 (b) KidStock/Blend Images/Getty Images; 138 (bg) Image Copyright Joan Kerrigan, 2013 Used under license from Shutterstock.com; 138 (inset) iStockphoto.com/Hallgerd; 139 Ken Seet/Corbis; 141 James Hardy/PhotoAlto/Corbis; 142 KidStock/Blend Images/Corbis; 143 Bill & Peggy Wittman; 144 Providence Collection/Licensed From Goodsalt.com; 145 Tim Pannell/Corbis; 146 Anderson Ross/Blend Images/Corbis; 148 Image Copyright Joan Kerrigan, 2013 Used under license from Shutterstock.com; 149 Tim Pannell/Corbis; 154 (c) Christopher Futcher/the Agency Collection/Getty Images; 154 (b) IS2 from Image Source/Alamy; 155 Bill & Peggy Wittman; 158 VINCENZO PINTO,VINCENZO PINTO/AFP/Getty Images; 159 Bill & Peggy Wittman; 160 (tl) AP Photo/Michael Sohn; 160 (tr) AP Photo/Gregorio Borgia; 160 (bl) Thierry BOCCON-GIBOD/Gamma-Rapho via Getty Images; 160 (br) AP Photo/Osservatore Romano, HO; 161 Tetra Images/Corbis; 162 (bg) Image Copyright Joan Kerrigan, 2013 Used under license from Shutterstock.com; 162 (inset) Bill & Peggy Wittman; 163 VINCENZO PINTO,VINCENZO PINTO/AFP/Getty Images; 166 (l) imagebroker/Alamy; 166 (r) Friedrich Stark/Alamy; 167 Manor Photography/Alamy;

168 SuperStock/Getty Images; 169 Our Sunday Visitor; 170 (t) Stephanie Maze/CORBIS; 170 (b) Jon Feingersh/Blend Images/Corbis; 172 (bg) Image Copyright Joan Kerrigan, 2013 Used under license from Shutterstock.com; 172 (inset) david tipling/Alamy; 175 SuperStock/Alamy; 178 Our Sunday Visitor; 179 David Litschel/Alamy; 180 plainpicture/PhotoAlto; 182 (bg) Image Copyright Joan Kerrigan, 2013 Used under license from Shutterstock.com; 182 (inset) KidStock/Blend Images/Corbis; 183 David Litschel/Alamy; 188 (c) iStockphoto/Thinkstock; 188 (b) Great crowds followed Jesus as he preached the Good News, 2004 (w/c on paper), Wang, Elizabeth (Contemporary Artist) Private Collection/© Radiant Light/The Bridgeman Art Library; 189 Cultura Creative/Alamy; 194 Bill & Peggy Wittman; 196 (bg) Image Copyright Joan Kerrigan, 2013 Used under license from Shutterstock.com; 196 (inset) Meg Takamura/Getty Images; 197 Cultura Creative/Alamy; 200 Bill & Peggy Wittman; 201 moodboard/Corbis; 202 Tom Grill/Tetra Images/Corbis; 204 Mike Kemp/Rubberball/Corbis; 206 Image Copyright Joan Kerrigan, 2013 Used under license from Shutterstock.com; 207 moodboard/Corbis; 210 Our Sunday Visitor; 213 Bill & Peggy Wittman; 214 iStockphoto.com/asiseeit ; 216 (bg) Image Copyright Joan Kerrigan, 2013 Used under license from Shutterstock.com; 216 (inset) The Sacred Heart of Jesus, end of nineteenth century (mixed media), European School, (19th century)/Private Collection/Archives Charmet/The Bridgeman Art Library; 217 Our Sunday Visitor; 222 (c) iStockphoto/Thinkstock; 222 (b) Kurt Vinion/Getty Images; 223 Jos Mensen/Foto Natura/Minden Pictures/Corbis; 224 Bill & Peggy Wittman; 225 iStockphoto.com/TerryHealy; 230 (bg) Image Copyright Joan Kerrigan, 2013 Used under license from Shutterstock.com; 230 (inset) Bill & Peggy Wittman; 231 Bill & Peggy Wittman; 236 iStockphoto.com/nano; 237 Bill & Peggy Wittman; 238 Janine Wiedel Photolibrary/Alamy; 239 OJO Images Ltd/Alamy; 240 (bg) Image Copyright Joan Kerrigan, 2013 Used under license from Shutterstock.com; 240 (inset) Our Sunday Visitor; 241 Bill & Peggy Wittman; 243 Bill & Peggy Wittman; 246 Corbis; 248 (cl) Bill & Peggy Wittman; 248 (cr) Our Sunday Visitor; 248 (b) Bill & Peggy Wittman; 250 (bg) Image Copyright Joan Kerrigan, 2013 Used under license from Shutterstock.com; 250 (inset) Robert Harding Picture Library Ltd/Alamy; 251 Our Sunday Visitor; 256 (c) Ocean/Corbis; 256 (b) Monalyn Gracia/Corbis; 258 Jeff Preston/Licensed From Goodsalt.com; 259 Ocean/Corbis; 260 Elio Ciol/Corbis; 261 (t) NOAH SEELAM/AFP/Getty Images; 261 (b) Bill & Peggy Wittman; 262 Jose Luis Pelaez, Inc./Blend Images/Corbis; 264 (bg) Image Copyright Joan Kerrigan, 2013 Used under license from Shutterstock.com; 264 (inset) plainpicture/Pictorium; 265 Elio Ciol/Corbis; 267 Dean Conger/Corbis; 269 (l) iStockphoto.com/asiseeit; 269 (r) Flint/Corbis; 270 Radius Images/Corbis; 271 Jim West/Alamy; 274 (bg) Image Copyright Joan Kerrigan, 2013 Used under license from Shutterstock.com; 274 (inset) iStockphoto/Thinkstock; 275 iStockphoto.com/asiseeit; 277 (bg) Fuse/Thinkstock; 277 (inset) iStockphoto/Thinkstock; 278 (bg) keith taylor/Alamy; 278 (l) iStockphoto/Thinkstock; 278 (r) iStockphoto/Thinkstock; 279 Standard Publishing/Licensed From Goodsalt.com; 280 Cameron/CORBIS; 281 Zvonimir Atletić/Alamy; 282 Jon Feingersh/Blend Images/Corbis; 284 (bg) Image Copyright Joan Kerrigan, 2013 Used under license from Shutterstock.com; 284 (inset) Stockbyte/Thinkstock; 285 (bg) Fuse/Thinkstock; 285 (inset) iStockphoto/Thinkstock; 290 altrendo images/Getty Images; 292 Our Sunday Visitor; 294 Mario Tama/Getty Images; 296 (l) JLP/Jose L. Pelaez/Corbis; 296 (r) Album/Art Resource, NY; 297 St. Vincent de Paul (1581-1660) 1649 (oil on canvas), Bourdon, Sebastien (1616-71)/St. Etienne du Mont, Paris, France/The Bridgeman Art Library; 298 Tom Payne/Alamy; 299 Arnel Manalang/Alamy; 300 Tim Gainey/Alamy; 302 altrendo images/Getty Images; 303 (t) iStockphoto/Thinkstock; 303 (cl) iStockphoto/Thinkstock; 303 (cr) iStockphoto.com/maribee ; 304 Jim Whitmer; 305 Photo by Franco Origlia/Getty Images; 306 Scala/Art Resource, NY; 307 Fred de Noyelle/Godong/Corbis; 310 Our Sunday Visitor; 311 (l) Jacek Bakutis/Alamy; 311 (r) Arterra Picture Library/Alamy; 315 (l) Tanisho/Alamy; 315 (r) Prayer card depicting 'Our Lady of Guadalupe', c.1900 (colour litho), French School, (19th century)/Private Collection/Archives Charmet/The Bridgeman Art Library; 319 Pascal Deloche/Godong/Corbis; 323 Our Sunday Visitor; 324 Our Sunday Visitor; 326 Our Sunday Visitor

Music selections copyright John Burland, used with permission, and produced in partnership with Ovation Music Services, P.O. Box 402 Earlwood NSW 2206, Australia. Please refer to songs for specific copyright dates and information.

English translation of "Morning Prayer," "Prayer Before Meals" (Retitled: "Grace Before Meals"), and "Prayer After Meals" (Retitled: "Grace After Meals") from Book of Blessings. Translation copyright ©1988 by International Committee on English in the Liturgy, Inc. (ICEL).

English translation of "Come, Holy Spirit" (Retitled: "Prayer to the Holy Spirit"), "Prayer to the Guardian Angel" (Retitled: "Angel Guardian"), and "Angelus" from A Book of Prayers. Translation copyright ©1982 by International Committee on English in the Liturgy, Inc. (ICEL).

Twenty-Third Publications, A Division of Bayard: "Morning Offering" from 500 Prayers for Catholic Schools & Parish Youth Groups by Filomena Tassi and Peter Tassi. Text copyright ©2004 by Filomena Tassi and Peter Tassi.